The Cloak and the Parchments

The Cloak

and the

Parchments

FRANK SPINELLA

RESOURCE *Publications* • Eugene, Oregon

The Cloak and the Parchments

Copyright © 2009 Frank Spinella. All rights reserved. Except for brief quotations in critical publications or reviews, no part of this book may be reproduced in any manner without prior written permission from the publisher. Write: Permissions, Wipf & Stock, 199 W. 8th Ave., Suite 3, Eugene, OR 97401.

Resource Publications
A Division of Wipf & Stock Publishers
199 W. 8th Ave., Suite 3
Eugene, OR 97401

www.wipfandstock.com

ISBN: 978-1-60899-072-6

A majority of the Scripture quotations contained herein are from the New Revised Standard Version Bible, copyright © 1989 by the Division of Christian Education of the National Council of the Churches of Christ in the U.S.A. and are used by permission. All rights reserved.

Manufactured in the U.S.A.

This book is dedicated to my wife, *Linda*,
whose patience with me as I researched and wrote
for long hours into the night is just one example
among many of her love and support. As in everything
I do and have done, she has been my silent partner.

Acknowledgements

I wish to thank *Dr. Marvin Wilson*, Professor of Biblical and Theological Studies at Gordon College, whose helpful comments on an earlier draft of this book have made it both more historically plausible and more theologically consistent. Because it remains a work of fiction, any remaining inaccuracies in the book may perhaps be forgiven, but without exception they are mine, not his.

"But will God indeed reside with mortals on earth?"
2 Chronicles 6:18

Chapter 1

It was just after sunrise when I made my way down to the already busy Ephesian waterfront. The fishermen were long since out on their boats, hidden from sight by the early summer's morning mist. On the dock in front of the ship that was soon to bear me to Italy, a centurion stood speaking in Latin to the first mate, apparently going over the supply list. Not quite fluent in the language, I hoped their Greek was better than my Latin. Still, I would have Timothy with me; if need be, I could depend on him to serve as translator once we reached Rome.

Timothy! Where *was* he?

I was thankful that Timothy had been able to book our passage on such short notice, and with a military escort, at that. Our ship was a commercial vessel, a three-masted *navis oneraria* without oars, preparing to sail in the company of two Roman warships, which likely meant that there would be particularly valuable cargo on board. Galley convoys were the safest way to travel. In general, Rome had made the shipping lanes safe for trade over a century earlier; Pompey's campaign against the Cilician pirates in the Eastern Mediterranean had made sure of that. No serious challenge to Roman naval supremacy had been mounted since, and while piracy had not been entirely eliminated, attacks were mostly confined to unaccompanied cargo ships. "The Lord will protect us," Timothy had said. But a couple of fully-armed Roman galleys nearby couldn't hurt.

At length I spotted my traveling companion, coming down the main road to the harbor, his trailing donkey laden with two small trunks for our journey. I waved vigorously at him, and caught his smile as he recognized me. "You're late!" I shouted. His smile grew slightly impish in response.

Timothy was a small man, in his late thirties although he looked even younger. His demeanor was calm and even-keeled at all times, but with a presence that commanded respect befitting an acknowledged leader of the church in Asia Minor. He gave me an embrace and a kiss, and as I looked in his steely eyes I felt the worries of the morning evaporate. Timothy had that effect on people.

"We have not much time before we depart," he said. "Please attend to the trunks, Mark. I must speak to the . . . the . . . what is the proper word?"

"*Magister navis*," I informed him with a grin. The twinkle in his eye showed that Timothy was testing my vocabulary rather than asking for help, but I played along. "For one who grew up in Galatia, Timothy, your Latin leaves much to be desired; perhaps it would be best to address him in Greek!"

As Timothy strolled down to the dock to find the captain of our ship, he was recognized by several of the brothers, whom he quickly dispatched to assist me with the animal and our trunks. I thanked them for their help. There were a good many faithful believers in Ephesus; Paul had spent a number of years here, and despite his forced departure after organizing a mass burning of pagan writings right in the shadow of the Temple of Artemis, his teachings had taken root.

Nevertheless, I feared for the local church while Timothy and I would be away, perhaps for many months. The factions among us could easily grow more divisive without Timothy's presence, and more believers could be led astray, at least until Tychicus, dispatched by Paul to take Timothy's place, would arrive from Rome. Timothy had tried to reassure me that Paul would not have sent for us if he thought Tychicus and the elders could not shepherd the flock during our absence. I was less sanguine. Was this fear a reflection of my own wavering faith, my own latent doubts surfacing again? I could not be sure. But I hoped to use this trip to discuss a great many things with

Timothy. I looked forward to having him all to myself for a time, undistracted.

As we brought our things down to load on the ship, I felt a tingling excitement. It had been several years since my last and only trip to Rome. While Ephesus was itself a great city of over 200,000 souls and could justly lay claim to preeminence in the eastern Mediterranean as a trade and cultural center, it could not hold a candle to Rome.

Still, my excitement was laced with apprehension. Paul was once again in a Roman prison, awaiting a second trial on the sedition charges levied against him by his Jewish enemies. He had been imprisoned there once before, when I was last in Rome with him, but conditions were more uncertain now than they had been then. Priscilla and Aquila, recently arrived from Rome, reported that the Emperor Nero was increasingly coming under the influence of Tigellinus, his sinister prefect of the Praetorian Guard, and was becoming even more unstable, reviving trials for treason throughout the City. Rome was typically tolerant of most other religious groups, particularly of the Jews since Nero's marriage two years earlier to Poppaea Sabina, a Jewish sympathizer—but such tolerance was extended only if those groups refrained from proselytizing. Judaism was by and large not a proselytizing religion. Paul, however, was concerned with little else. In converting Jews, whom the Romans permitted to refrain from offerings to their gods in recognition of Jewish monotheistic culture, Paul committed no offense. But inducing Gentiles to deny the Roman gods or to reject the prevailing cult of emperor worship could certainly count as treason. The dangers could not be ignored, not by me at least.

Timothy, however, displayed no such concerns. "Come, Mark," he greeted me at the gangplank with a calming smile. "Let us give thanks to God, and ask his blessing on this journey."

We boarded the ship and each went down on a knee, heads bowed, as Timothy prayed aloud for fair winds and calm seas. My mind strayed as I felt the eyes of crew and passengers upon us. Less than a minute on board a Roman vessel bound for Italy, and already we had given ourselves away as Christians! But that, of course, was precisely what Timothy wanted. He planned to use the trip as an opportunity to preach the message of salvation to a captive audience, as many as would listen.

He couldn't know how much I myself needed that message renewed.

Chapter 2

Under full sail, our ship headed west into the Aegean as I watched two weathered and barefoot crew members scurrying from mast to rope to sail like a pair of monkeys. Amid the creaking of wood and the spray of salt water, the morning mist lifted and the sun peaked through breaks in the clouds. There was something about a sea voyage that heightened one's senses and brought forth a spirit of adventure in a way no land journey could.

We were making for the island of Delos, about halfway to the Greek mainland and, according to myth, the birthplace of Apollo and Artemis—and there to spend our first night. If the wind cooperated, we would easily arrive before sunset.

Timothy sat in the stern on top of his trunk, hunched forward with his arms around his knees as if trying to keep warm, although the salty air was already quite comfortable. As always, he seemed at peace. Nothing ever seemed to rush him into action—except for Paul's letter. Timothy had received it less than a week ago, advising that Tychicus would shortly be arriving at Ephesus and imploring us to come to Rome before the winter, yet here we were on our way without even awaiting Tychicus' arrival and with summer barely begun. Timothy had picked up on the sense of urgency between the lines of Paul's letter, and had no wish to risk a voyage later in the year, when wind and weather would be against us.

At length I interrupted his thoughts. Or perhaps his prayers.

"Thinking of Paul?" I inquired.

"Indeed I was," he replied. "He will be glad to have his cloak back before the winter."

"More so to have the parchments back."

"No doubt that is true. Whatever else may be stowed on board, this vessel surely contains no more precious cargo than the parchments. I am confident that God will suffer no calamity to befall this ship, lest they be lost."

I sat beside him, making myself as comfortable as I could. "Tell me, Timothy; do you think all of the things written in these parchments are true? What I mean is, have all these sayings of our Lord been recorded faithfully?"

"Why do you question it?"

"I don't, really. But how can we be sure? Memories fade with time. These are, after all, not contemporaneous records. And secondhand, at that."

"Always the cynic, Mark! Put your doubts aside; do you not recall Paul telling us that Peter vouched for their accuracy when he turned the parchments over to Paul? If you question whether the words attributed to the Lord were indeed spoken by him, what better attestation can there be than that of someone who walked with him, ate with him, conversed with him?"

"None, I suppose." My answer did not sound convincing even to myself. Timothy picked up on the tone of skepticism in my voice.

"Even in the short time you have been in Ephesus, Mark, have you not been troubled by those claiming special knowledge gleaned directly through supposed revelations from God, leading to modifications of the faith we have been taught? There are no ready means to test the validity of such claimed revelations; wouldn't you agree?"

"I would. And no means to disprove them, either," I added. "Just as there is no test to disprove the claim of a vision of the risen Christ, nor that such a vision was as true an encounter as that which Peter and the other disciples have had—and which distinguishes them as true apostles."

"Then how do we distinguish the truth from the lie? Surely we do best to rely on those whom the Lord chose, those who lived with him, traveled with him, to tell us what is consistent with his teachings—and to question the rest. Until he returns, and while the apostles are alive, *theirs* is the testimony that must be accepted on such matters. And when the last of them departs to be with the Lord, we who have received the faith directly from them, from the eyewitnesses to his teachings and miracles, must continue as guardians of the truth."

"You sound as though you are not expecting the Lord's return to be soon."

Timothy looked almost wistful. "I did once—when I first received the gospel from Paul. Back then, we all did." He stood, opened and reached into his trunk, and removed the parchments. "I'm sure you know the passage I am looking for," he said as he spread the parchments on the deck in front of us. "Here:

> *'I tell you truly, there are some standing here who will not taste death until they see that the kingdom of God has come with power.'*

Quite naturally, we took this to mean that the Lord would return in glory within a generation. Now, I think, it may be quite some time. Ours is not to know the hour—nor even the decade."

As Timothy returned the parchments to his trunk, I was suddenly puzzled by the writer's use of parchment, a medium designed to last for centuries, rather than the less durable papyrus, much cheaper and more readily available—and certainly quite sufficient for the purposes of a scribe who truly believed that all of his potential readers would pass away before his ink did! Had the writer suspected something that his contemporaries did not?

"Suppose, Timothy, that it is many years before the Lord returns, and our grandchildren's grandchildren are yet awaiting his coming. Will there not be more false claims, by more false teachers claiming to know the true path?"

"Certainly that is a danger. It is up to us to lay the proper path now with clarity, lest future generations be led astray. We must cling to the faith and the traditions we have been given. Paul and I have spoken often of this, and of the need for appointing successors who can be at the core of a structured church."

"Do you believe that the Lord so intended—I mean, to establish a structured church?"

"Not at all, Mark. His intention, I believe, was simply to reform Judaism and fulfill its promise, not to establish a new religion. Certainly the church in Jerusalem has remained true to Jewish traditions under James' leadership, and no doubt will continue to do so even now that James has passed on. But I believe the Lord also wanted to make Judaism more universal, as is shown by his willingness to associate with those who would be considered impure or lawbreakers. That set a precedent for our outreach to the Gentiles. Largely thanks to Paul, the gospel has spread to the Gentiles without importing the full panoply of Jewish cultural and religious restrictions. But that is precisely why some structure to the faith is needed."

"How do you mean?"

"If the gospel is truly to be universal, it must be preserved without alteration—and not just from regression into formalistic Jewish practices. There are other heresies and perversions to be reckoned with. As Paul's letter points out, there are those who refuse to tolerate sound doctrine, preferring to follow their own desires and to surround themselves with teachers who tell them what they wish to hear. The elders in Ephesus and elsewhere will require a central authority to turn to, to decry the false teachings of those who deem themselves inspired, but who deviate from the faith we have received. In my view, that authority can best come from the original apostles; it is they who lay the strongest claim to know the direct teachings of the Lord."

"Do you not include Paul in this group?" I asked. "Has not the Lord revealed himself as well to Paul—directly, as he tells it, while on his way to Damascus?"

"Even though I myself received the faith from Paul, I cannot include him, lest the same arguments levied against heretical teachers be used against him as well. He calls himself 'Apostle,' but his apostleship and his vision of the Lord came about in a different manner than those who were directly commissioned by the Lord before he ascended to the Father. 'Born out of the normal course,' as Paul himself put it in writing to the believers at Corinth. Paul should not set himself as a stumbling block by claiming primacy over Peter and the others on matters of the Lord's direct teachings."

"But isn't that precisely what he *has* done? You know of the disagreements he has had with Peter and the others in Jerusalem, and in Antioch. And you know well his frequent claims of authority over the churches throughout Asia and Greece—authority received directly from the Lord, as he puts it."

"Are we to split into factions, Mark, like the Corinthians that Paul chastised? There has been enough of that! We are followers of Jesus Christ, and no other. If, indeed, what Paul has received from the Lord is not in full accord with what Peter and the other apostles report that Jesus himself has said, then Paul must either convince them to interpret the Lord's words differently, or else defer to them—at least with respect to those matters which they have witnessed with their own eyes and heard with their own ears."

Although Timothy was certainly a disciple of Paul, I was not surprised to hear him defend the position that eyewitness accounts of Jesus' teachings must ultimately triumph over all contrary views. Logical argument was Timothy's greatest strength, with pragmatism a close second. The courage of his conviction that harmony among the brethren on matters of faith could be achieved by logical persuasion—something that certainly had not always been the case, as Paul's heated battles with the elders in Jerusalem had proven—was firm enough now to stand up even to a personality as dominant as Paul's. How I longed to have even a small measure of that conviction!

"And when this generation has passed away, and none of the Twelve are left alive, what then?" I asked. "Are they to appoint successors who will preserve the truths that they have witnessed—to the exclusion of all contrary teachings?"

"How else can it be, Mark? What other guardians of the truth can hold such authority as those who have received the word directly in succession from one who received it from the Lord? There is no text, no written exposition of the Faith to refer to in resolving such disagreements."

"We do have the parchments," I suggested. "And copies of letters that Paul has sent to the churches throughout the region."

"But those letters are literally all over the map, Mark. They were all written to believers who had *already* been taught the Way, and for that reason they make no serious effort to recapitulate those teachings, as opposed to exhorting believers to hold fast to the teachings previously received. Moreover, each such letter is specific to its own unique context. I was with Paul when he dictated letters to the churches at Thessalonica, Philippi, Corinth, Rome—and each time, he wrote to address whatever pressing issues were at hand in a particular church at a particular time. Do you recall the disruption of worship being caused by those women in Corinth some years ago? Paul wrote to the Corinthians that women should remain silent in such gatherings; yet a few years later he sent Phoebe, a deaconess of the church in Cenchreae just a few miles from Corinth, to preach in Rome!

"My point is that we would be hard-pressed to distill a consistent and complete explication of the faith simply through Paul's letters, even if there were a dozen more of them. And anyway, as we have said, Paul lacks the eyewitness perspective. The parchments may have that benefit, but they are likewise scattered fragments of our Lord's teachings."

"Then it should all be written down as a coherent whole," I suggested. "While eyewitnesses are still alive, *their* testimony should all be written, for all to refer to, until the Lord returns. The sayings recorded here in these parchments—they should be woven into an account of his ministry and of his revelations of the Father."

Timothy nodded his agreement. "You are a good writer, Mark. With all of the reading you do of Greek mythology and plays, one might even call you a scholar! Have you ever thought that perhaps you have been called for just such a purpose, to write such an account?"

"No, Timothy, not I. I was but a young lad in Jerusalem when the Nazarean preached there, and I never heard him speak even once. What little I know of his ministry I have learned from Peter, James and the others. Surely it is Peter who would be best suited for this task."

"I do not disagree with you. But Peter is no writer; perhaps you could be of aid to him in that regard."

"If that were truly God's purpose for me, then why am I going to Rome? Is not Peter in Jerusalem?"

"Patience, my brother! Wherever he is, if it be God's will that you meet up with him, you shall. Rome will not be your last journey in the service of the Lord. And besides," Timothy continued with a wink, "Who is to say whether Paul's request for your presence is not related somehow to your writing?"

Chapter 3

We anchored at Delos as the sun was setting, and Timothy went ashore to assist in bringing on fresh water and provisions. I stayed on board, and by the light of a single lamp I spread the parchments before me on top of Paul's cloak. It was too dark to read them easily, and I quickly replaced them.

My thoughts turned to Paul. We had had our differences in the past, but I knew that each time the fault was mine. In Pamphylia, I was not ready for the trials that I knew would await us, and I had abandoned Paul there, returning to Jerusalem with my faith shaken. I could not blame him when later, in Antioch, Paul refused to let me accompany him on his next mission, despite the pleadings of my cousin Barnabas. Years later, when we were in Rome together, Paul dispatched me to Colossae, but sent Tychicus ahead of me bearing a letter suggesting that I might or might not arrive.

The truth was that I lacked the unwavering zeal that Paul and the others had for preaching the Way to the Gentiles—and Paul knew it. Yet now he wanted me with him again. But why?

Even now, I questioned my own faith. When I first received the gospel as a youth in Jerusalem years ago, directly from Peter, it was rapturous and transforming—but over the years my conviction had often waxed and waned. Paul's insistence that all believing Gentiles were the new Israel, the true people of God, flew in the face of my traditions, and to this day regularly shook my confidence. At times I even questioned whether Paul was letting his own ego get the best of him. He saw himself as the new Jeremiah, to whom God had said 'Before I formed you in the womb I knew you, before you were born I dedicated you, a prophet to the nations I appointed you.' Paul had written the same of himself, in virtually the same words, to the Galatian churches years ago. Was Paul coloring the gospel as he saw fit in order to cast himself in that role? Did he teach the radical proposition that baptism was the equivalent of circumcision solely to gain favor with his Gentile audience?

If this was truly the good news that we must preach, how could one such as I, prone to bouts of doubt and fear, truly be of service to the Lord? Did I love him less than the others? I marveled at their strength of conviction, and felt inferior in my inability to sustain that same conviction.

Timothy was a ready reminder of my inadequacy. Though younger than I and a newer convert, he was a born leader, an eloquent and fearless spokesman for the salvation in Jesus Christ—and in more recent times, Paul's most trusted personal emissary. Although his mother was Jewish, his father was Greek, so Timothy was not raised as a Jew; yet at Paul's suggestion he had been circumcised as an adult in order to help him gain acceptance with the Jews in Asia—something I surely would never have done! All of the elders in Ephesus and elsewhere in Asia looked upon Timothy as a pillar of the faith, despite his relative youth. How did they look at *me*, I wondered?

Still, the thought of helping to write an exposition of the Lord's teachings did appeal to me, and I let myself dare to imagine that I might have been called to do exactly this. As a Jew, I understood the importance of the scriptures. Since the Diaspora throughout the Greek world, the Jewish religion was of necessity the religion of a book. John the Baptist aside, no true prophet had appeared in Israel for centuries, yet it was the written word, and the law given to Moses, which had served as the linchpin of Jewish belief, study and worship throughout the Mediterranean world for centuries. The Torah, the Nevi'im and the Kethuvim, as well as scholarly commentaries and interpretations of them, were central to being a Jew, particularly a Pharisaic Jew, and it was difficult for me to imagine religious life without them. In time, similar writings could be equally central to the religious life of a Christian. But was I truly fit for so important a task?

Timothy's return to the ship interrupted my thoughts. "We are to sleep on board tonight, Mark," he called. "If you need to stretch your legs ashore, now is the time."

"In a minute," I replied. "First, I must ask something of you."

"What is it?"

"Pray with me, Timothy. Pray with me for the strength to hold fast to the service of the Lord."

Timothy looked genuinely concerned. "Tell me what is troubling you," he urged as he sat on the deck next to me. "I can see in your countenance that there is turmoil in your soul."

"The turmoil is in my mind more than my soul, Timothy. You know that I am given to doubts, to questions about the salvation we have received in the Lord. I have this consuming need to understand it in logical terms, to have it all make sense, to have it be rational. Yet faith and rationality seem with me always to be at odds, always incompatible. Constantly I am looking for proof. If God is testing me, I confess I am acquitting myself poorly!"

"One's beliefs would hardly be a matter of 'faith' if precise proof were readily available, would it? No matter; tell me what you *do* believe to be absolutely true. Perhaps we can build from there."

"I believe that God is One: the God of Abraham, Isaac and Jacob, He who created the Universe. I believe that He has given the Law through Moses to a chosen people with the free will to accept it or reject it. I believe that His covenant with Israel was that there would be a reward reserved for those who live according to His will. I believe that He has appointed Jesus of Nazareth as His anointed one, to institute a new covenant, one which is written on the hearts of men. I believe that God's promised deliverance of Israel from its sufferings has occurred in His vindication of Jesus as the suffering representative of Israel, that He has raised Jesus from the dead as proof that the new covenant he has brought to us is indeed the way to eternal life. I believe that the new covenant is inclusive of Jews and Gentiles alike. And I believe that God will keep His end of the covenant and gather for eternity all those who have kept *their* end."

"And of what are you *un*certain?"

"Of the precise terms of this new covenant. Of the continuing value of Jewish law. Of the nature of Jesus and his relation to God. Of the Messiah's rule, as prophesied. Of a *hundred* things, Timothy! I have so many more questions than answers."

"Then we shall endeavor to explore those questions and answers together. But tell me this first, Mark. When you first came to believe, did you not feel the joy, the transforming power of God's love in the very depths of your being?"

"I did indeed!"

"Then use that feeling as your guide for what is true. Our bodies and souls do not lie to us. If an answer *feels* right in that same way, if it gives you that same sense in the depths of your being of something true, you must promise me you will not reject it merely because you lack sufficient other evidence from which a logical or rational proof may be drawn. Are we agreed on this?"

"Yes, yes, agreed! Oh Timothy, I had so hoped to discuss these things with you on the voyage. Thank you! This will be most appreciated!" I could hardly contain my excitement. "Where shall we begin?"

"With that prayer you asked for," Timothy replied in his usual calming manner. "And a good night's sleep."

Chapter 4

I awoke to the stirring of the crew as it made ready for our departure. We were heading southwest for Melos, an island with a tragic history. As recounted by Thucydides, Melos had initially been sympathetic to Sparta during the Peloponnesian war. The Athenians sent envoys to Melos to persuade them to fight instead with Athens, or else be annihilated by superior numbers. When the Melians offered instead to remain neutral, the Athenians besieged the island, massacred the men, enslaved and deported the women and children, and resettled the island with Athenian colonists.

Sitting in the stern as we got underway, I could still feel the rise and fall of the ship, although much less than in the bow. A few meters away Timothy was already talking about the Way to one of the passengers, a Cretan merchant whom we had met the day before. Saving souls was never far from Timothy's mind at any time of the day or night.

At length Timothy finished the conversation by embracing the man, and then turned back toward me with a nod and a smile. "This man knows Titus and some of the faithful in Crete. By God's grace, he is coming to believe! I must write Titus to welcome him on his return. That, however, can wait until after we eat; I am starved!"

We made ourselves as comfortable as possible, and over our breakfast of wheat cakes and pears, I could barely wait to open the conversation we had started the previous day. But Timothy was his usual relaxed and unhurried self. At last he seemed ready to talk. "All right, Mark. Where shall we begin?"

"Let us speak first of the new covenant, the one foretold by Jeremiah. What are the details of this promise by God, and what performance does He require of us in order to obtain it?"

"Mark, you seem to want to define all the terms of this new covenant as though it were a contract produced by many lawyers! Let us simplify the question if we can. Is your question not simply this: what must one do in order to be saved?"

"That does capture the kernel of my meaning, yes."

"And should we not first define salvation, define being 'saved,' before we attempt to answer this question?"

"I agree."

"I think you have touched on the meaning already, Mark: eternal life with God. Is that not what you meant—life eternal, precisely as our Lord has promised?"

"It is. Of course I still expect to die one day, but the hope of a life *after* death, at least in a spiritual if not physical realm, in a paradise of joy and happiness with God and His angels—*that* is what I mean."

"You say the *hope* of eternal life, Mark—not the *certainty* of it. Are you unsure whether your soul is immortal?"

"As a matter of pure logic, I confess I am unsure. I struggle even with the notion of a soul as existing independent of a body. The Genesis story teaches that man was a physical body fashioned from the earth and *then* animated by the breath of God, not a soul or spiritual being which was then incarnated in flesh. So why should we think that the soul can exist independently of the body?"

"Your body is made up of composite parts, each of shape, mass and function—skin and bones, organs and sinews, blood and other fluids, and so on; is it not so?"

"Indeed."

"These parts can corrupt and die, whether by natural or unnatural causes—and indeed, if the more vital of these parts are separated from the whole, death of the whole is sure to result, is it not?"

"True."

"But what of the soul? Does it likewise consist of composite and divisible parts?"

"No."

"Can that which is not composite be dissolved, or that which is indivisible be divided?"

"It cannot."

"Is it not then logical to say that the soul, being spirit and not corporeal, being incomposite and not the sum of parts, need not be affected by the same corruption and destruction which overtakes our physical nature?"

"I agree, Timothy. On the other hand, the soul seems always to be associated with one body, dependant upon it as its vehicle, so it would not be illogical to conclude that when we breathe our last, our souls may cease to exist as well, for want of a vehicle to carry them further. Either could be true, as I see it."

"This 'paradise of joy and happiness' that you say you hope for; like every human being, you want at all times to be happy, do you not?"

"Of course."

"Can you achieve complete happiness within the span of your physical life, to the point where you are fully sated with happiness and wish for no more?"

"We will always want more happiness, Timothy! Happiness is not something that we can say one day, we have had enough of! It is human nature always to want more happiness."

"Then tell me, my logical friend: do you think God would implant in human nature a desire that could never be fulfilled? Would that not be inconsistent with your notion of a perfect, loving and just God?"

"I suppose it would be inconsistent."

"So there must be a way to achieve this perfect and sufficient happiness that by nature all men desire; don't you agree?"

"Yes, I suppose so."

"Well, if during the entire span of our lifetime we do not achieve it, do not stop wanting more happiness, then unless we are to say that God has instilled in us a craving that can never be sated—which we have agreed is not logical—there must be a possibility of life beyond the grave where this perfect and sufficient happiness may be enjoyed, must there not?"

"That would make sense, Timothy, but for one thing: at every moment *after* death, would we not still want more happiness the next moment, and the next . . . and so on to infinity—so that this craving can *still* never be satiated, even in heaven?"

"Ah, so on to infinity, you say. I see." Timothy had that thoughtful gleam in his eyes as he paused, and looked askance for a moment. "I think, perhaps, that you and I mean different things by the phrase 'eternal life'—or perhaps I should say that our notions of 'eternity' are different."

"How so?"

"By your answer, Mark, I glean that you are equating 'eternity' with 'perpetuity.' To me, the two concepts are not equivalent. To me, 'eternity' suggests an unchanging, immutable and therefore timeless state, while 'perpetuity' suggests a temporal component, that is to say, everlasting, for all time, for an infinite duration of time. Do you understand the distinction I am drawing?"

"Perhaps you should explain it further."

"My notion is simply that time is nothing more than a measure of change. Think of it this way: If all were static—if the universe were completely motionless—then rational, sentient beings within that universe would have no conception of time. So it is one thing to say that after the body dies, the soul lives on in perpetuity, for all time; that would entail the notion of everlasting existence in a universe of change. It is quite another to posit that after the body dies, the soul remains for eternity, unchanging and immutable, outside any realm that can be measured by time—or space. To the extent that it is eternal, then, the soul would be as free of the temporal dimension as of the physical dimension—and equally free of dependence on the physical and changeable body."

"Ah! Now I see the distinction."

"And do you also see which is better able to be fully happy and need for no more: a soul that thereafter experiences change, or one that does not?"

"The latter."

"So if, after death, the soul experiences no 'next moment,' but only an eternal 'now,' would you then agree that this desire for happiness, insatiable while we live in the flesh, could indeed have been instilled in us by a just, loving and perfect God, without the logical objection that your notions of infinity and perpetuity entail?"

"I would agree."

"And let us look at this from the opposite perspective. Tell me, Mark; do you believe not only in heaven, but in hell?"

"I do. I think of hell as a place—perhaps I should say a 'state'—of eternal punishment for the wicked."

"But during a man's life, no matter how extensive his wicked deeds, surely he can only have been *finitely* evil, not *infinitely* so—at least as you reckon infinity; am I right?"

"You are."

"If God is indeed just, then, surely He would not mete out infinite punishment for finite evil, would He?"

"I suppose not."

"Then a place or 'state' of eternal punishment cannot be consistent with the notion of a just God—if 'eternity' is simply 'temporal infinity.' Agreed?"

"Agreed."

"So whether in terms of heaven or hell, must we not say that eternal life is indeed different than perpetual life?"

"We must, if we are to believe God to be just."

"Precisely, Mark. And if such a concept of eternal life follows rationally from the concept of a just, loving and perfect God, should we not also explore God's justice, love and perfection for clues as to how eternal life is to be obtained—what you have been calling 'salvation?'"

"I am anxious to do so!"

"We have agreed that it is not illogical for the soul to survive the body and enjoy eternal life—but neither is it necessary that all souls *will* do so. I take it, by phrasing your question as one of 'salvation' you mean 'being saved from the *absence* of eternal life'—saved from eternal death, in other words?"

"True."

"So, if one needs to be 'saved' from eternal death, then such eternal death must be what awaits us if we do *nothing*, if we keep *no* covenant with God; else the concept of 'salvation' would make no sense here, would it?"

"No."

"Eternal life, then, is not the automatic fate of all humanity simply by virtue of being born; rather, the status quo, if not altered, leads to death. Is that not your belief?"

"It is."

"And it is this altering of the status quo through the promises of our Lord—the 'new covenant,' as you phrased it—which you wish to understand better, so that you will know how one may secure the promise of life eternal that awaits those who keep their end of the 'bargain,' as you put it?"

"Exactly!"

"Then let us look first to the old to give context to the new. As you have said, it was with Israel that God made the old covenant, to be their God and to take them as His people, called apart from the rest of the world. And as you have said, obedience to the Law of Moses was what He demanded of Israel, in return for which He offered—what?"

"As the Torah puts it, 'to raise them high in praise and renown and glory above all other nations he has made.'"

"Do you understand this to be the same as eternal life?"

"In truth, Timothy, I am not sure. The Torah makes no mention of eternal life, not explicitly anyway. It references 'salvation' only in the context of deliverance of Israel from its enemies, and in the context of a long and prosperous life followed by an unending line of descendants."

"Then unless such references are a euphemism for eternal life, the old covenant is different from the new on *both* sides—that which God offers, and that which man must do to demonstrate acceptance; do you agree?"

"I do indeed. But if these words *were* meant euphemistically, if they were intended to have a meaning beyond the literal, why the obscurity? Why would the scriptures not be direct, if this were their true meaning, rather than casting something so important in metaphor?"

"Why indeed, Mark! What shall we say, then? That a faithful Jew who observes the Law in every respect has earned God's favor for himself and his progeny so long as they shall live, but does not have the promise of life eternal in God's presence as his reward?"

"It would seem so."

"And indeed, that is what the Sadducees believe. But the Pharisaic view is quite different; to varying degrees, they hold to life eternal as the reward for faithful observance, do they not?"

"It is as you say; the Pharisees interpret the Psalms, certain of the Prophets, and the apocalyptic books, particularly the Book of Daniel, as supporting the promise of eternal life for those who adhere to the Law."

"But as we have said, this is not a necessary interpretation. And even if it were a defensible one, still, the *quid pro quo*—faithful adherence to the Law—is at best a difficult achievement, perhaps an impossible one given the frailties of human nature; is it not so?"

"It is. There are so many precepts to keep, and the Torah is explicit that one who fails to fulfill any of the provisions of the Law shall be accursed."

"Is it likely, then, that God would be so mean-spirited as to set before His people so precious a prize, yet at the same time ensure that it is virtually if not completely unattainable?"

"I cannot believe that He would!"

"It must follow, then, that the Pharisaic interpretation must be wrong; that eternal life is not a reward for faithful observance of the Law, and indeed never was. Do you agree?"

"Yes, that follows."

"At least in terms of the promise of eternal life, then—whatever other benefit there may have been, and may still be, to being a descendant of Abraham and to observing the Law—there is no advantage to being a Jew. For purposes of gaining eternal life at least, Jew and Gentile are on an equal footing."

"So it seems."

"And perhaps we can be even more general: If even observance of the Law—the very precepts for behavior given by God Himself as a commandment to His own chosen people—does not have as its reward eternal life, then perhaps eternal life is not strictly a reward for human behavior at all. After all, had God intended eternal life to be a *quid pro quo* for the performance of some set of humanly achievable acts or forbearances, surely it would have been to Israel that such a reward for conduct would have been offered; don't you agree?"

"I do."

"And if it is not a reward, eternal life must then simply be a gift; does that not follow?"

"I suppose it does. Still, I cannot believe that our actions are of no concern to God, that He does not care how we behave, or whether we lead just and moral lives."

"Nor do I make any such claim, Mark. Certainly He cares! And we shall return to this subject in due course. For now, I simply mean to draw the distinction between *earning* salvation as a reward for a moral life, and receiving salvation as the unmerited *gift* of God."

"I see the distinction. But if, indeed, eternal life is simply a gift, who receives it, and how?"

"To this subject, we will turn in earnest tomorrow. For now, however, let us break from our discussion. See, we are approaching Melos!"

Chapter 5

Early the next morning our convoy departed Melos and headed southwest to Cythera, opposite the southern tip of the Peloponnesian peninsula, and according to legend the island of Aphrodite, goddess of love and beauty, who was carried there on a giant sea shell. The sea was choppy, but again with a tailing wind that strained at the sails and creaked at the timbers of the ship. This stretch of the journey was a bit longer than yesterday's; we would need favorable winds throughout the day if we were to make the island before darkness.

After a breakfast of cakes and honey, Timothy was ready to indulge my inquisitiveness again, and began the conversation. "We were speaking yesterday of the distinction between earning eternal life, and receiving eternal life as a gift; were we not?"

"Yes. And I questioned, on whom is the gift bestowed."

"Ah, yes. To answer your question, let us begin by asking, what else is there besides a person's conduct which can serve as a basis for having this precious gift bestowed upon him? What, aside from how one lives one's life, would induce God to extend that life beyond the grave? If not one's *actions*, it must be one's *beliefs*, must it not?"

"That would certainly make sense. It would naturally be those who believe in God who are most likely to gain His favor, if that is what you mean."

"But let us be more specific, Mark. To believe 'in' God is too amorphous. What, precisely, is it *about* God that must be believed? Simply that He exists? Or something more?"

"In truth, it must be something more—yet I am not sure that I could compile a complete list of the propositions that must be believed. I suppose the first such proposition must be that He is One, and supreme over all creation."

"Ah, but the Torah already teaches *that*—yet as we have agreed, its precepts are not sufficient for one to gain eternal life. Focus on His gift, Mark—on what must be believed *about* His gift. Must we not start with the proposition that eternal life *is*, indeed, a gift, and not something we earn through our actions?"

"You mean, accepting the notion that eternal life cannot be earned through our actions is itself a prerequisite to receiving it?"

"That is my meaning precisely—giving up the prideful belief in eternal life as a reward for one's conduct opens one to the possibility of receiving it. Is this not the point of the story recounted in these very parchments, regarding the man who approached Jesus to ask what he must do to share in eternal life?"

"What do you mean?"

Timothy reached into his trunk for the parchments, and spread them before us. "Here," he gestured. "Read with me:

> 'A man asked him, "Good Teacher, what must I do to inherit eternal life?" Jesus answered, "Why do you call me good? No one is good but God alone. You know the commandments: 'You shall not murder; You shall not commit adultery; You shall not steal; You shall not bear false witness; You shall not defraud; Honor your father and mother.'" He said to him, "Teacher, I have kept all these since my youth." Jesus answered, "You lack one thing; go, sell what you own, and give the money to the poor, and you will have treasure in heaven; then come, follow me." At this, the man left in sadness, for he had many possessions.'

Do you understand, Mark? No human is 'good' so as to merit eternal life, nor is keeping the commandments enough to result in one's own salvation. One must instead have faith that God will provide that salvation."

"But was not this man told to give all his possessions to the poor? That seems to me to refer to *actions* he needed to take; and if he did, he would be saved."

"Yet by giving away his worldly goods, would not this man be demonstrating complete faith in and reliance on God, rather than on himself?"

"I suppose that is so."

"And here, Mark, we see the relation between faith and action. If a man truly believes something, he then will act as though it is true. Our very lives attest to this. If we believe it will be a cold day, we dress for the cold; if we believe that fire burns us, we refrain from touching fire; and so on. Is it not always thus?"

"Undoubtedly."

"So, if this man had truly believed in Jesus as the way to salvation rather than in his own obedience to the Law, he would have divested himself of his possessions and gone with Jesus, would he not?"

"That follows."

"Then by his actions, or rather inactions, he demonstrated that he lacked the faith that was necessary to save him, did he not?"

"I would have to agree."

"And looking closer, his lack of trust in Jesus' approach to salvation is mirrored by a reluctance to give up what he had accumulated on his own; he wished to continue his self-reliance, to trust in *himself* rather than to let go of those things and trust completely in God. In a word, we may say his was the sin of pride; do you agree?"

"Yes."

"So it is in every case where one relies on one's own efforts. In the end, the sin of pride is always the truly deadly sin. As the Proverb puts it, 'Pride goes before destruction, and a haughty spirit before a fall.' It is precisely what Paul meant when he first wrote: 'Salvation is yours through faith. This is not of your own doing; it is God's gift; neither is it a reward for anything you have accomplished, so let no one pride himself on it.'"

"I agree, Timothy. It is pride we must overcome." I quickly shrugged aside the thought that Timothy might have had *me* in mind when saying this. More likely, the truth was simply hitting close to home.

"And what is the opposite of pride, Mark? Is it not humility?"

"Yes."

"And if we have humility, will we not then, and only then, be able to trust completely in God, who alone can bring us to eternal life?"

"Yes, Timothy. I see. So then, the second proposition that must be believed to be true is that salvation is a matter of God's grace, and not of man's individual achievement. What is the next?"

"To find the answer, let us look anew at this same passage—at the meaning of Jesus' admonition that *'No one is good but God alone.'* If God alone is good and perfect, and man therefore is not, how is the sinful to partake of the good? Must there not be forgiveness of sin in order for man to share in the goodness and perfection of God?"

"That is only logical."

"And how is sin forgiven? Do not the Scriptures teach that it is by blood, by a sacrifice?"

"That is so; the Book of Leviticus instructs that it is blood shed on the altar that makes atonement for our lives, as blood contains life. But I must confess, I have always found this to be most troubling. To accept that without the shedding of blood there can be no forgiveness of sin entails belief in an exacting, vengeful God whose own forgiveness, and therefore whose own love, is conditional. Yet we have been taught that God's love is *unconditional*."

"We have been taught correctly, Mark; but you confuse unconditional love with unconditional forgiveness. All forgiveness must be conditional on *something*; for if forgiveness were automatic, sin and absence of sin would be of like effect, would they not?"

"I suppose so. But why should forgiveness be conditioned on *sacrifice*, of all things?"

"Let us consider your question by noting two aspects of the animal sacrifice that is prescribed in Leviticus—the victim's vicarious bearing of the sins of the offeror, and the offeror's giving up something of value. What is the symbolic meaning of the first aspect? Is it not to reinforce the notion that death is the penalty for sin?"

"Surely."

"And is this death penalty not simply God keeping His word, keeping the bargain He made with Adam, that if he disobeys God by eating of the forbidden tree—the metaphor for sin—death will result?"

"I suppose it is."

"Insisting on fulfilling a bargain cannot be unjust, can it?"

"No."

"And if God also affords us a means of sparing the true sinner's life through the vicarious sacrificing of an animal, that justice is tempered with mercy and love as well, is it not?"

"I see your point. God, being just, is not releasing us from our bargain, but He is deeming it satisfied vicariously."

"Well, temporarily at least; we will come back to that in a moment. But now let us turn to the second aspect of sacrifice, that is, the giving up of something of value. Tell me: when one has wronged his neighbor in some way, is it not justice to require of the wrongdoer some recompense to make his neighbor whole, simply as restitution, and wholly apart from any motive of vengeance or retribution?"

"I agree."

"And will not that recompense, that restitution, require some giving up of value, some sacrifice on the part of the giver?"

"Certainly."

"Then once again, to condition forgiveness of sin on sacrifice for that sin may as easily demonstrate God's justice, and not His vengeance; do you see?"

"Yes; I see your point."

Timothy reached anew for the parchments, and spread them before us. "Here," he pointed and read aloud:

> *A leper came to him, and kneeling before him beseeched, 'If you will to do so, you can make me clean.' And Jesus touched him and said, 'I will it; be clean.' Immediately the leprosy left him, and he was cured. And Jesus said to him, 'Go and show yourself to the priest, and offer for your cure what Moses has prescribed.'*

Even here, Mark, our Lord's miracle, although occasioned by the leper's faith and belief, was nevertheless followed by the command that the sacrifice prescribed by the Law must still be offered."

After all the times I had heard Paul insist that even Jewish believers were free of the strictures of the Law, this passage gave me pause. "But that is what I do not understand, Timothy. Why was the leper's faith alone not enough to merit forgiveness and cure from an unconditionally loving God, without further offering of sacrifice?"

"Perhaps the answer is best found by considering your objection that God's love must be unconditional, side-by-side with the notion of God's justice in requiring the death penalty as a sacrifice in discharge of sin in fulfillment of the bargain made with Adam. Do you not see how the two notions can be harmonized?"

"Tell me."

"If God Himself were to provide the sacrifice—just as Abraham said to Isaac on their way to Moriah—surely that would demonstrate His love, would it not?"

"No doubt it would."

"And if that sacrifice were truly an ultimate one, akin to that which Abraham was preparing to make of Isaac, surely then it could be said that God's love was truly unconditional, could it not?"

"Assuredly; I cannot think of a greater sacrifice than the life of one's only son."

"Then forgiveness through sacrifice is fully consistent not only with God's righteous demand that the ancient bargain be fulfilled, but also with God's unconditional love for the forgiven—provided that God furnishes the sacrifice and that the sacrifice is sufficiently great, such as, for example, with the gift of God's son."

"I am constrained to agree."

"Do you recall what our Lord said about himself as a sacrifice?" Timothy spread the parchments before us again, and began perusing them. "Here," he gestured:

> *'I have come not to be served but to serve, and to give my life as a ransom for many.'*

If, then, Jesus is truly the Son of God, his sacrifice would satisfy your concern regarding the harmonization of God's unconditional love and His forgiveness, would it not?"

"It would; but how can it be just for God to impose punishment and sacrifice on one for the sins of another?"

"Your point is well taken, Mark, but not your premise; for if Jesus *voluntarily* submitted to the punishment and sacrifice, we can no longer say that it was imposed upon him by God, can we?"

"No."

"And is that not the import of what we have just read?"

"I suppose it is." I was suddenly struck anew with wonder over how great must have been Jesus' love, to take on such an ultimate sacrifice voluntarily. I imagined him conflicted as the hour approached, yet bending to the will of his Father. I imagined him praying, *Father, you have the power to do all things. Take this cup from me. But let it be as you will, not as I will.*

Timothy continued on. "Are we agreed, then, that God's justice and His love would be merged in the sacrifice of His only Son as atonement for man's sins?"

"We are. But is that the true import of our Lord's death, Timothy? *Is* he truly the Son of God, literally rather than metaphorically, begotten rather than adopted? How could he be God, yet human? And, must we believe this in order to be saved? We must talk more about this!"

"And tomorrow, Mark, we shall." Timothy had that familiar calmness in his voice again, unhurried and at ease. "But let us stop for today."

With that, Timothy yawned. How he could possible be tired, how he could fail to be stimulated by this discussion to the point of excitement, was beyond my ability to fathom—unless it be that with wisdom there comes a certain serenity. Timothy was far and away the most serene person I had ever encountered. And serenity cannot easily be shaken.

Chapter 6

Our next destination was Pylos on the western coast of the Peloponnese—and according to Homeric legend the city of King Nestor, the wise elder statesman of the Greeks who sailed against Troy, and who later hosted Telemachus during his quest to seek out his father Odysseus. We were heading north now; the wind would be less full in the sails, perhaps requiring some tacking.

My own sails, however, were still full of yesterday's discussion, and the promise of greater understanding today. I had hardly slept, analyzing the arguments Timothy had made. As I turned them over and over in my mind, it occurred to me that I was looking for flaws in his logic with dogged determination, chipping away at it as one would chisel against a rock. It was almost as though I did not want logical proof to be available, as though I wanted to continue doubting. While a part of me wanted desperately to believe purely on faith without benefit of rational proofs, that part was losing out. Again.

What *was* this thirst for logical proofs that haunted me and made me feel so inferior in faith to Timothy and the rest of the brothers? Why could I not hold on to the passionate certainty that I had felt in my heart when I first heard Peter preach the Word two decades ago?

Timothy sat next to me in the stern, silently watching the sail billowing, appearing deep in thought. I knew that look—and knew not to interrupt it. At length he spoke. "I have been thinking through the night," he said, "of how best to describe Jesus' nature. It is difficult to do, for I am convinced that he has a dual nature, that of both God and man—although at first blush one nature would appear to exclude the other. This is what you wish to understand, Mark, is it not—how one can simultaneously be both the son of God and son of man?"

"That is precisely my question. As I believe, God has no body; God is pure spirit, uncreated, always existing, existing before there ever was a physical world—a physical world which God created. I see it as inconsistent for an incorruptible and immortal spiritual being to have flesh and blood, bone and sinew, which by nature corrupt and die."

"Ah, just as I thought," Timothy smiled. "You see the dilemma as one of logical impossibility, Mark."

"What do you mean, *logical* impossibility?"

"I mean an impossibility which follows from the very definition of the terms used. For example, even presuming that God is all powerful and can do anything, He still cannot make a square circle, nor make a stone so heavy that even He cannot lift it, yet these 'inabilities' are not true limitations on His omnipotence, because they are mutually exclusive *by definition*. Do you see?"

"I think I do."

"These physical qualities of man you mention, having corruptible flesh, blood, bone and sinew—you would agree that they are separate from the quality of a man's soul or spirit, and not of its essence?"

"Of course."

"And indeed, we have already posited that the soul can have life beyond the physical life of the body, haven't we?"

"We have."

"A soul could logically be clothed with mortal flesh, even on a human plane, then, without destroying its essence?"

"That follows."

"And may we define 'man' as a being having both a body and a soul, the one physical and corruptible, the other spiritual and incorruptible?"

"We may."

"Similarly, your objection to Jesus' being both God and man was that God, as a pure spirit, is eternal and incorruptible; must we not also say that God's spirit, no less than man's, could logically be clothed with mortal flesh without destroying its essence?"

"No doubt that is so."

"Then the partaking of a divine spirit and a human body at once is not of the character of *logical* impossibilities; which is to say, it is not inconsistent *by definition*. Agreed?"

"Agreed."

"So, if a divine spirit in a human body is not *logically* impossible, then it must be within an omnipotent God's power to achieve, must it not?"

"In those terms, Timothy, I would agree; nevertheless, I would say that the divine spirit and the human soul are truly different even if both be capable of eternal life—for the one is created, the other does the creating, existing from all time prior to all creation. If Jesus was created, was born into the world, then I cannot see how he could also be *un*created God."

"You have begged the question, Mark! You have presumed that Jesus was created in respect of both body *and* soul. But that need not be the case."

"Explain."

"To be truly human, created in the flesh, he would of necessity have been born of a woman, would he not?"

"Yes."

"To be truly divine, uncreated spirit, he would of necessity have been begotten directly of God, would he not?"

"Again, yes. But how can both be possible?"

"It is written by the prophet Isaiah, '*the virgin shall conceive and bear a son, and shall name him Immanuel.*' I contend that that this prophecy has been fulfilled in Jesus."

For an instant, I was taken aback; the possibility of the passage's reference to the birth of Jesus had never occurred to me. I had always translated the Hebrew word *almah* to mean *young girl at the age of puberty* rather than its alternative translation *virgin*—and had presumed that the son referred to in this passage was Hezekiah, the son of King Ahaz to whom this prophesy was made. Who could blame me? The notion of a divine father and a human mother was popular in Greek mythology and legend, but quite foreign to Judaism. There was, of course, the metaphorical reference early in the Book of Genesis to the "sons of God" taking wives from among the daughters of men prior to the Great Flood and producing the race of giants known as the Nephilim, but I had always understood those "sons of God" as being angels, and not true deities.

Timothy must have seen the look of puzzlement on my face. "Suspend your disbelief for a moment, Mark, and consider: if God, being pure spirit, were ever to take on flesh and become one of us, how could it be otherwise than by a virgin birth? For if the seed of a man had caused Jesus to grow in his mother's womb, then he would have been born *simply* human, and not the son of God at all. He would, being man, have had to *become* God at a later time—which we have agreed is illogical."

"I must confess, I had never considered that."

"And let us go further: being begotten *of* God need not mean being created *by* God, but merely emanating *from* God—and all the while *of one being* with God. Do you see this as well?"

"I must ask you to elaborate, Timothy."

"We spoke earlier of time as a measure of change, and of the distinction between everlasting existence in a universe of change, and the eternal 'now' which does not change; do you recall?"

"I do."

"Is ours not a temporal universe of change?"

"Assuredly so."

"And is God's?"

"Assuredly not; He is unchanging."

"In our world, if a man creates something, there surely was a point in time when he existed but his creation did not. Is not that the nature of creation; creator always precedes creature in time?"

"Of course."

"Similarly, if a man procreates, he must of necessity have existed in time prior to his child, must he not?"

"I agree; although perhaps we may say that the seed which became his child was always present within him, or at least latent within him."

"Yes, but even there, would it not be accurate to say that the latent or potential child is surely different from the actual child, which comes to be what we properly describe as a child later in time?"

"True."

"But if, in God's world, all is immutable and time has no application, would it not be contradictory to speak of a prior 'time' when God existed, yet that which emanates from Him did not?"

"It would be. But could not the same argument be made as to any of God's creations? This world, for example: if God created it, must it not, by the same logic, always have existed?"

Timothy's wry smile widened slightly. "You beg the question, Mark. Before God creates a *changeable* universe, there is nothing to which time can apply; true?"

"I suppose that is so."

"Then the universe that God created would not always have existed, nor was there a point in 'time' when He created it, God Himself being timeless; do you see?"

"I think I do."

"If a son of God exists—by which I mean a being begotten of God so as to be fully of His essence—he will likewise be timeless, will he not?"

"Yes."

"Then that which emanates from God—a son begotten of God—could not have been created, but was (and is) eternally a manifestation of God. In such a timeless realm, the son exists, but did not *begin* to exist; he always was. Would that not follow?"

"It would."

"Is it not then also logically possible that God intervened in our changeable, created world, at a point in *its* time, by sending His son into the world to take on human form?"

"Certainly."

"Can we now agree, it *is* possible that God took on a mortal human form in the person of Jesus, without compromise of His divine essence—including the essential quality of not being created?"

"I will agree."

"Now let us look at this mystery from the opposite side: If God can partake of our humanity, is there any sense in which man can partake of God's divinity?" Timothy paused briefly, a pregnant pause for effect, giving me to know that something important was about to pass his lips. "Perhaps here, Mark, you may find an answer to your questions about salvation."

I could feel the joy of discovery descending on me, like a child experiencing the thrill of learning how to read, or to solve arithmetic problems for the first time. I recalled Timothy's admonishment when the voyage began: if an answer *feels* right, if it yields that same sense in the depths of my being of something true as when the Way was first shown to me, I must trust it, and embrace it regardless of logical proof. Timothy's explanations were *feeling* right.

I didn't want the feeling to wane. "Tell me more," I pleaded.

Timothy, however, displayed no sense of urgency in exploring the subject further. "Soon, soon. But we have had enough discourse for now, my brother. I have promised our new friend, the Cretan merchant, that I would spend some time to speak with him of the Way—and I see him waving to us!" With that, Timothy arose and went aft.

Instead of following him, I went at once to the trunk and took out the parchments again, perusing them for some confirmation of what I had just heard from Timothy. If Jesus was truly God, had he claimed to be such? There were several scattered sayings in the parchments in which he referred to himself as the "Son of Man," but none directly as "Son of God." But there was one which at least hinted at his acknowledging being both:

> 'For whoever is ashamed of me in this sinful generation, of him will the Son of Man also be ashamed, when he comes in the glory of his Father with the holy angels.'

As I pondered the meaning of these words, it occurred to me that Jesus may have been invoking a parallel to a passage in the Book of Daniel:

> *In my vision at night I looked, and there before me was one like a son of man, coming with the clouds of heaven. He approached the Ancient of Days and was led into his presence. He was given authority, glory and sovereign power; all peoples, nations and men of every language worshipped him. His dominion is an everlasting dominion that will not pass away, and his kingdom is one that will never be destroyed.*

Had Jesus used "Son of Man" as a euphemism for "Son of God," perhaps in order to avoid the direct claim to divinity which could be used against him by his enemies?

Chapter 7

At sunrise the next morning we set out into the Ionian Sea, bound for Cephalonia, the largest of the Ionian islands, named for the mythical hero Cephalus, fabled Athenian hunter who mistook his wife for a deer and killed her with a magical spear that never missed its target. There we would bring on fresh provisions, as well as new goods and new passengers, for the remainder of our voyage.

I had practically roused Timothy from his sleep, and he could hardly have helped sensing how anxious I was to continue our discussion. Yet he maintained his unhurried composure, as serene as ever. As he went aft to stretch his legs, I turned and leaned against the top wale of the ship, gazing toward the horizon, smelling the salt and feeling the spray of the sea as the ship rose and fell with each wave. This journey, I knew, would end all too quickly, and what awaited us in Rome I could only guess. If I was to be truly useful to Paul, I was running out of time to conquer the self-doubt that had plagued me.

When Timothy returned, it was with the countenance of a man on a mission.

"Where did we leave our discussion of yesterday, Mark?" Before I could answer, he exclaimed "Ah, yes! How man may partake in God's divinity, wasn't it?" With that, he stood up abruptly, making his way to our two trunks we had stowed in the stern of the boat. I followed dutifully.

Timothy reached in one of the trunks, and produced a round loaf of bread, a tin plate and a small bronze cup from beneath Paul's cloak—giving me to know that it was time for the Eucharistic meal. "Bring the wine, Mark," he instructed, motioning with a nod of his head toward a sheepskin flask we had brought, sitting atop the other trunk.

Then Timothy promptly walked toward the benches at the rear of the main mast, where the boatswain was seated, taking a break from his duties on the ship. He had been watching us intently for some time.

"May we join you, sir?" Timothy asked as he seated himself directly next to the man, not waiting for an answer. He motioned me to sit across from him, and I complied, with no protest from the boatswain.

"You are Christians," he said to Timothy and me. "Are you not?"

Timothy showed no trace of surprise as he pulled a stool from under his bench, and setting it as a table between us, placed the plate on it and then the loaf on the plate. "Indeed we are, sir; but tell me, how did you know this?"

"Since we left Ephesus I have observed you," he replied. "I see that you are devout. The two of you pray often, but you cannot be true Jews, for you do not ritually wash your hands before you eat."

"You are most astute, sir. And what do you know of *our* rituals?"

"Little enough. You do not eat meat which has been sacrificed to other gods. You have a rite of initiation, I am told, involving immersion in water. Beyond that, I do not know."

"Then perhaps you would like to observe another ritual, one we are commanded to perform in memory of our Lord."

With that he placed the loaf of bread in front of him and prayed over it, saying the words that had grown so familiar to me: "We thank thee, our Father, for the life and knowledge which thou hast made known to us through Jesus thy servant; to thee be the glory for ever." He then broke it and gave a piece to me, saying "Take and eat the body of our Lord." He ate the remaining piece, and then poured out some wine, again praying over it, saying "We thank thee, our Father, for the holy vine of David thy servant, which thou hast made known to us through Jesus thy servant; to thee be the glory forever." Then he passed me the cup, saying "Take and drink the blood of our Lord." I drank from the cup, and then passed it back to Timothy to finish. We then bowed our heads and gave thanks aloud, together: "Thanks be to thee, holy Father, for thy sacred name which thou hast caused to dwell in our hearts, and for the knowledge and faith and immortality which thou hast revealed to us through thy servant Jesus."

The boatswain, after watching this, looked bemused. "Surely you do not believe what you say about this bread and wine being flesh and blood."

"Why do you doubt it, sir?" Timothy asked.

"Because it is clearly not someone's flesh and blood you have consumed, but mere bread and wine."

"What appears to you as mere bread and wine, sir, has been transformed into something else. Reality and appearances, as Aristotle has shown, are not always the same."

The boatswain's bemusement turned to impatience. "But there is no evidence here of any such transformation. And even if it were as you have said, the very notion is disgusting! Is yours a religion of cannibalism?" Shaking his head, he abruptly got up and left us.

"It is difficult doctrine," Timothy mused aloud. "He does not understand it."

"I am not sure *I* understand it," I replied. "For all the years I have participated in this ritual and partaken of the bread and wine in solemn communion with other believers, I have taken on faith that the meal was more than merely commemorative of our Lord's sacrifice, that I was consuming his real flesh and his real blood. But I have never quite grasped how the transformation takes place. The taste and consistency are, after all, the same as any simple bread and wine I may eat."

"A food's taste and consistency are accidental qualities, Mark, not of its essence or substance. The food and drink you consume become a part of you, and give your body physical nourishment, independently of how they taste or feel, do they not?"

"They do."

"Why, then, should you judge their ability to give your *soul* spiritual nourishment by such accidental qualities?"

"I understand that much, Timothy. And in truth, I *feel* my soul nourished, even now, after consuming the blessed meal. But is the spiritual nourishment simply a function of the consumer's faith that the bread and wine have such effects, or is there a real transformation of bread and wine into a different substance—the body and blood of our Lord?"

"The transformation is real enough, Mark. Your faith does not make it so; your faith is the belief that it *is* so. It is God Himself who makes it so. Yet it is by faith that you appropriate the benefits of the transformation, for if you did not believe that the bread and wine had become spiritual nourishment, it would not be spiritually nourishing for you."

"Then whether it is the faith of the believer alone, or the actual intervention of God producing a change of substance that renders the bread and wine spiritually nourishing, the ultimate effect seems indistinguishable. Either way, it seems the faith is needed to secure the benefit."

"That is true, but misses the point. We cannot make something so simply by believing it to be so."

"Why, then, do we need faith in the transformation at all in order to enjoy its benefits? If the bread and wine are the true body and blood of our Lord independently of our faith that it is so, could not a nonbeliever such as this boatswain obtain the same spiritual benefits of the meal simply by eating with us?"

"The beliefs of the worshippers are no less important for their inability to bring about any change in substance, Mark. For example, we do not eat meat which has been sacrificed to idols, although its characteristics are unchanged by that sacrifice, because to partake of it would amount to confessing communion with idolaters. Similarly do we eat the bread and wine that has become the sacrifice of our Lord's body and blood to confess communion with all believers, although that confession does not convert bread and wine into flesh and blood. The difference between the meat sacrificed to idols and the bread and wine which recalls the sacrifice of our Lord involves precisely what we were discussing earlier—the sense in which man can partake of God's divinity."

"Explain."

"Tell me, my Jewish brother: what is it, above all else, that unites all Jews everywhere, whatever their place of birth, language, or vagaries of their individual beliefs?"

Surprised though I was by the question, I did not need to think for even a second to come up with the answer. "The sacrifice regularly offered in the inner court of the Temple on Mount Zion."

"And what is sacrificed there? Is it not the flesh and blood of an unblemished animal?"

"Yes."

"And for whom is that sacrifice offered? For Jews only, or for Gentiles as well?"

"Only for Jews, Timothy. The sacrifice is prescribed by the Law, and Gentiles are not bound by the Law. Paul's teachings have made *that* much consistently clear, I would think." Only later would I think of the *in*consistency with this teaching that Paul had exhibited in having Timothy himself circumcised. But Timothy, the ultimate logician, made no mention of it here.

"Then what is the sacrifice which unites Christian believers as well? Is it not our Lord's death?"

"I have no doubt of it."

"And how are these believers to partake of that sacrifice? Can there be a better way than in consuming the very bread and wine—the very flesh and blood—which commemorates that death, and having consumed it, allow it to become a part of our very bodies?"

For a moment, I was without words; all I could do was nod my assent.

"Let us go further: is it not a commandment of the law of Moses—indeed, from the time of God's admonition to Noah—that blood must never be consumed?"

"That is so; the blood of an animal is deemed to contain its life essence, which belongs to God. Thus no animal killed by strangulation may be eaten, for such means of slaughter leaves blood in the meat. As it is sacred to God, all blood must be poured out and not be consumed."

"Yet our Lord commands us to drink his very blood—a sharing, then, in *his* life essence. But only if he is truly God will his blood, his life essence, represent *eternal* life, and allow those who consume it to partake of that eternal life. And since God is pure spirit and not flesh and blood, it was necessary for God to become incarnate for this to occur. It was necessary for God to take on flesh and blood, and for God-become-man to become the sacrificial lamb, to accomplish this."

Once again I could only nod my agreement; I was far too excited by Timothy's insight to speak.

"Do you not see it all, Mark? Man's sharing in the divine essence; Christ as God-become-man; his death as a sacrifice for the sins of man; the bread and wine as his flesh and blood; the communion of his church; all are facets of the same single truth, the same identity!"

My pulse was racing! I knew to a certainty that Timothy's words contained a great and transforming message. I did not want to lose the moment, but somehow I knew that I needed time to digest what I had just heard. It was as though pieces of a puzzle had been thrust so close in front of my eyes that the picture they formed could not come into focus without a step back. Although putting them into a coherent whole was all that mattered to me at that moment, I knew the moment could not be rushed.

Timothy obliged me, albeit unknowingly. "We will discuss this again later, Mark," he said as he rose. "But right now, I must speak further with the boatswain."

This was to be a night of very little sleep for me.

Chapter 8

In the morning we headed north again toward the island of Corcyra, named for the beautiful nymph with whom Poseidon fell in love. According to Homer, this was where Odysseus had washed ashore after being shipwrecked, the penultimate stop on his twenty-year journey back to Ithaca. If the winds for our crossing were favorable, it would also be our final stop before heading to Brundisium in southeastern Italy.

After eating a few of the corncakes and cheese we had brought on board at Pylos, Timothy and I were ready to resume our discussion, and again made our way to the stern of the ship, sitting with our backs to the cross-breeze out of the west, which was particularly strong today, creaking the timbers of the boat as it titled off the wind. Today, Timothy seemed even more anxious to open the conversation than I—albeit with a question that I did not expect.

"Do you feel the love of God, Mark?"

My hesitation in answering so simple yet disarming a question was fueled by equal parts of surprise and embarrassment. "I . . . I . . . often do feel it, yes. Yes, of course, Timothy!" My words did not sound convincing to myself, and I was sure that they did not convince Timothy, either.

"Tell me, then: what does it feel like?"

It was obvious that Timothy was looking for a more profound answer than I could muster on the spot, but I fumbled as best I could.

"Peace, contentment, thankfulness for good fortune, being blessed with good health . . ."

As I spoke, Timothy closed his eyes and shook his head, two fingers on his temple, putting himself in the wrong to ease my difficulty. "No, no, that is not my question—or rather, I've asked the question too broadly. These feelings you describe are accidental qualities that may perhaps be generated from any number of sources. What I meant to ask is, can you describe the unique experience of God's love, in terms of His presence in your life? How do you know it is *God*, it is *His* love, that you feel when you say you feel it?"

Gathering myself, I paused for a reflective moment, and responded. "There are times—rare moments, to be sure—when I have sensed the presence of a power beyond my comprehension, when I have felt somehow connected to something so much greater than myself that I can only stand in awe. The feeling might be brought on by just about anything, from a beautiful vista to the funeral of a loved one. At those times, I have been suddenly overwhelmed by a peace, a serenity that cannot be adequately described. Inevitably the feeling wanes and quickly leaves, becoming an exquisite yet fading memory, leaving behind a hope, even a longing, for the next encounter. It can scarcely be put into words. Are those the words you ask me for now, Timothy?"

"Yes! That is it precisely! Do you understand such experiences as being given a brief taste of union with God?"

"I suppose that is one way to put it, although 'union' may be putting it a bit strongly."

"Not too strongly at all, Mark. You hesitate to express this feeling in terms of union with the Almighty because you have been imbued in the Jewish view of God as so supreme, so fundamentally different and other than created, sinful man that it is blasphemous even to hint at the possibility of a union with God."

"No doubt I am a product of my culture; you must forgive me!"

"I do. Yet I am convinced that that union is exactly what the experience of God's love is about."

"How do you mean?"

"I mean no more than that the goal of love is always union with its object."

"Explain."

"Let us analogize to love on a human plane, for example in a marriage. Marriage is the undertaking of a *way of life* in which two people commit to each other, foregoing other liaisons, and forging a union to fulfill each other's emotional, physical, and social needs as best as they can—and in this way forming a spiritual bond; is that not so?"

"Certainly."

"If I 'love' my wife, do I not then seek union with her, emotionally and physically; do I not seek to form that spiritual bond, to become a 'unit' not only in social and economic terms but in spiritual terms?"

"Yes."

"For us to love God, and for God to love us, must similarly entail the forging of such a union; do you not agree?"

"I suppose I must agree, but I still see union with God as a very different thing."

"Tell me how."

"In a marriage I see, hear and touch my mate—indeed, I can be completely physically intimate with her—and this reinforces the experience of spiritual union. In a relationship with God, the physical senses do not translate the experience of union. If it cannot be sensed, I do not see how something can be experienced."

"Yet you have just described for me those fleeting, rapturous moments when you have become awestruck by the power of a presence beyond yourself; is that not an experience of spiritual union akin to, if not on a level beyond, what is experienced in marriage?"

"That is so."

"Then the physical senses cannot be strictly necessary to the experience of a spiritual union, can they?"

"I suppose not."

"And how does one come to achieve spiritual union with a spouse? Is it not through the way of life embodied in the marriage, a longstanding appreciation of the mutual commitment, sharing and sacrifice made by the partners to the union over an extended period of time?"

"I am sure you are correct."

"My belief is that our experience of union with God comes about in much the same way. Over time, an *appreciation* of the love, commitment and sacrifice of God-become-man in the person of our Lord simply translates into the experience of spiritual union as a living reality."

"But such love seems so one-sided," I objected, "not at all as in a marriage."

"Ah, Mark, but it is still a love that calls for a response! We have, after all, been commanded to love God with our whole heart, mind and soul."

"True; but is such love even possible for any human being?"

"If it is not, then we have not improved much on our Jewish roots; we will still have been given a law which cannot be perfectly kept! No, Mark, if Jesus came to perfect the Law, this commandment must be more than a goal to strive toward but ultimately fall short of. He must have given us the tools to accomplish the task, or more precisely—for 'tools' improperly suggests that reaching the goal is something that we can accomplish through our own efforts—He must have provided us with a way of experiencing that kind of perfect love; do you not agree?"

"I do. But what *is* that way, Timothy?"

"I believe it is to be found in a proper understanding of the incarnation, death and resurrection of Jesus as God-become-man. To understand the meaning of those events, and to appropriate their meaning into a present consciousness of union with God, we must first see Jesus as the embodiment of God's relationship to man, or more generally, of God's relationship to creation."

"Explain."

"A while ago, we were speaking of your religious and cultural bias against any view of God forging a spiritual union with mankind; do you recall?"

"Yes."

"Your notion that God and man are so fundamentally distinct as to preclude any possibility of spiritual union; is this not based on your view of God as sinless and mankind as sinful?"

"It is."

"Ah." Timothy paused briefly, as if for effect. "We must find a way for you to overcome that notion."

"Why? Is God not sinless, and is man not sinful? Indeed, did we not speak earlier of the sacrifice of God's own son as the perfect means for forgiveness of sin?"

"Indeed. But if you continue to view the distance between sinless God and sinful man as existing solely because of the sin, will you not then place your entire focus on the forgiveness of sin, on the sacrifice made by our Lord on the cross, as the exclusive means of experiencing union with God?"

"I suppose so."

"Then your focus is too narrow, Mark. By focusing on the crucifixion, you miss seeing the birth of the God-man as itself bridging the gap between God and man—the concurrence of Godhood and manhood that has been brought about by the incarnation of God in the person of the man Jesus of Nazareth. It is his *birth*, not his death, which first joined together the divine and human essences so as to make man's union with God palpable in the first place!"

This was something that Paul, focused always on the cross, had never spoken of, at least not to me. "Please explain," I urged.

"Throughout history, when mankind has tried to understand God as creator, the created and the uncreated have been viewed as incompatible by nature. This view of two substantively different beings, the One so transcendent and the other so contingent, is a hindrance to the proper understanding of the relation between God and man."

"How so?"

"For one thing, by ignoring the extent to which the Creator's essence is *already* immanent in His creatures. Do you recall God's answer when Moses asked God what he should tell the Israelites was God's name?"

"*Eheyeh asher Eheyeh.* 'I am who I am,' or 'I am He who exists.'"

"And do you see that in asking for God's name, Moses was asking for a description of God's very essence?"

"Yes."

"So by this answer, did not God declare that His *essence* is existence?"

"I agree."

"And it is precisely here, Mark, that insisting on the 'otherness' of God obscures a deeper truth regarding the '*isness*' of God. Creator and creature are different, to be sure—God's existence is necessary, whereas ours is not—but the fundamental nature of God as the very source of existence itself, as pure Being, is one in which *all* beings, all that exists, must of necessity partake in some measure."

"That makes sense."

"And would it not be fair to say that man, made in God's image and possessing an immortal soul, possesses an even greater measure of this essence than other creatures?"

"That is fair."

"And let us go further: if God and man were by nature incompatible, would it not be logically impossible, as we have earlier defined that notion, for God and man ever to have become united in the person of Jesus?"

"Certainly."

"So then, the union of God and man *is* possible, is it not?"

"I must agree. If we accept that Jesus was literally the Son of God, not in any metaphorical sense, we must accept the possibility of union of the divine and human natures."

"It remains for us to understand how that possibility of union becomes a reality for the rest of us," Timothy expounded. "And here we must ask: is there a true separateness between God and man as a result of man's sinfulness, which awaits the expiation of a sacrifice before it may be bridged? Or is that perceived separateness a distortion of a higher reality which man's sinfulness simply prevents him from recognizing?"

"I sense from your tone, Timothy, that you maintain the latter!"

"You sense correctly, Mark. I believe that God is within all of us, if only we have the wisdom to see Him there. And tomorrow, I will do my best to explain precisely how. But the evening is descending, and it is time for prayer. Look there; I believe I see the lights of Corcyra in the distance!"

Chapter 9

The next morning brought clear skies and steady winds out of the east, and as we made our way onto the ship, the Captain announced his intention to cross directly to the Italian peninsula rather than head further up the coast to Apollonia, where the Adriatic was at its narrowest. This would mean our first all-night sail of the journey.

Although I was anxious to continue our dialogue, Timothy was preparing for this final leg of our sea voyage with an extended time of silent prayer, and I had no wish to disturb him. I waited until we were well underway and the sun fully above the eastern hills before pressing him.

At length Timothy turned his attention to me. "Shall we continue our discussion of yesterday, Mark?"

"I would like nothing more," I replied.

"We were speaking of whether there is a true separateness between God and man as a result of man's sinfulness—or whether man's sinfulness prevents him from experiencing the reality of union with God that is innate within us; were we not?"

"Precisely."

"Then today, I have a contention to put forward—and let me confess up front that I cannot prove it logically—but you must promise not to judge it too quickly, not until we have finished. Are we agreed?"

"We are."

"I contend that divine transcendence and divine immanence are not incompatible notions. I contend that the experience of unity with God is latent within each human being, and that one of its effects is our innate moral sense, our awareness of the difference between right and wrong. Those who habitually choose the moral path—love of God and neighbor—thereby encourage this latency to surface, and eventually become conscious of their union with God. Those who habitually choose the immoral path—love of self, pride—do not."

Timothy paused briefly to study my reaction, and then continued. "Suppose that my thesis is correct. Would it not follow that if ever a man were truly and completely sinless, which is to say utterly selfless and solely devoted to the love of God and his fellow man, his would be the immediate consciousness of unity with God?"

"That would follow."

"And has Jesus not shown himself to be utterly selfless and devoted to the love of God and man, even to the point of death on the cross?"

"Certainly."

"Then would we not expect him to declare, without the slightest doubt or hesitation, that 'I and the Father are One?'"

"I would expect so. Yet nowhere in the parchments is any such declaration to be found—and surely, if our Lord had so declared, it would have been recorded there, Timothy."

"Perhaps; unless he was obliged to keep silent so as to hide that truth from his enemies. His experience, nay certainty, of unity with God, would have sounded so blasphemous to his audience at the time that it may have been unwise for him to utter the words."

As Timothy said this, I recalled having pondered the same possibility a few days earlier when considering the phrase "Son of Man" that appeared so frequently in the parchments; but I made no mention of this to Timothy. "It seems, almost, you are saying that our Lord was no different than the rest of us, except for a higher consciousness of union with God—and that we all could experience such union if only we could achieve that kind of love," I commented, with a bit of apprehension.

"In a way, Mark, yes; but as we have discussed earlier, I believe that our Lord was also divine by nature, an uncreated spirit, existing both *with* and *as* God before becoming incarnate. Our sharing in the divine nature is a created one, imparted through the very act of creation in God's image. His is a *necessary* unity with God; ours is a *contingent* one. Surely he *was* different from the rest of us, in a way which enabled him to experience union with God directly—in scriptural terms, to see the face of God directly."

"What do you mean?"

"Do you recall how Moses asked to see God directly in all His glory, and was told by God that no man sees the face of God and lives; so God covered Moses' eyes with His hand as He passed, and then let Moses see His back only?"

"Of course; meaning, as all Jews are taught, that God allows man to see Him only through His creations, which reflect His nature." I recalled what Paul had written in one of his letters to Corinth: *Now we see indistinctly, as in a mirror, but when we come into the perfection of His kingdom we shall see Him face to face.*

"You have been instructed well, Mark. But given his divine nature, the intimacy of his eternal relationship with the Father, surely our Lord was able to see the face of God in all of its glory. Yet as to his *human* experience of union with God, I see no reason to presume that his consciousness of union must have been essentially different from our own. Certainly it was more constant and more intense, given his selfless devotion and willingness to make such an ultimate sacrifice, but not different in kind on a human plane. Those rare and fleeting moments of rapturous presence you mentioned earlier when I asked you about experiencing the love of God; just imagine having that experience *all the time*, and perhaps you will have some approximate notion of the consciousness of union that our Lord must have had."

"But how can any ordinary human being ever approximate our Lord's experience of union with God, Timothy? Must we not live completely sinless lives in order to reach that stage of consciousness?"

"Not at all, Mark. If our sins are forgiven—which is the point of his death, as we have seen—and if we then strive toward the same love that he had for us, we can eventually come around to the same place, whether in this life or the next. God surely must recognize that our human frailties could serve as obstacles to such love, must He not?"

"I have no doubt of it."

"Does it not make sense, then, for God to have given us a source of strength to help us overcome them?"

"It does."

"And here is the beauty of the gift of His Son in the flesh, to help us overcome those frailties. For I am convinced, Mark, that it is not our Lord's death alone which makes this possible for us, but his life—a life that continues on in us, and we in him, when we come to appreciate and express our communion with him, in prayer and particularly in the Eucharistic meal."

"Explain."

"You are what you eat, Mark; food and drink become part of you physically, and as we have discussed earlier, spiritually—because a labor of love is entailed. The bread and wine we consume is the product of human toil; we grind the wheat and crush the grapes so that their earlier form is destroyed, but changed into something greater. God's labor of love effects an even greater transformation of that bread and wine, by an even greater sacrifice, so great that it is not the original form that is changed, but the very substance—and when *it* is consumed, that *substance* becomes part of our own. Partaking of the body and blood of our Lord with true belief in its nature expresses our solidarity with him, appropriates the healing benefits of his sacrifice, communes with his essence and makes it our own.

"Do you see? Holiness is not a matter of our individual achievement, but rather of relatedness to God, and the Eucharistic meal is a way of actualizing that relatedness. If we take Him not merely into our bodies but also into our hearts, we will of necessity adopt a spirit of humility, shun sin, practice love, and eventually realize the spark of the divine within us and flame it into fire. *That* is what leads to salvation, to eternal life."

Timothy paused, perhaps to let me digest his remarks, perhaps because there was nothing more profound to be said. Once again did I sense in my gut the truth of what was said. It *felt* right. I prayed that the feeling would not wane. And Timothy promptly obliged me with another pearl.

"I asked you earlier whether you felt God's love; do you recall?"

"I do."

"You described it as a fleeting awareness of the presence of a power beyond your comprehension, a connection to something greater than yourself, overwhelming you with a feeling of peace and serenity."

"That is right."

"And do you recall our earlier discussion that the goal of love is union with its object?"

"I do."

"What you characterized as God's love, I would characterize as God Himself, within you. He is there, in all of us, and the feeling of peace and serenity you described are but the byproducts of being in harmony with the living God who dwells within."

"But if God dwells within us, why then is it so rare for us to experience such bliss?"

"Because we so easily become distracted by the *world*, Mark! There are, at every turn in our daily existence on earth, so many distractions, so many things to throw us out of that harmony—bodily discomforts and sickness, preoccupation with earning a living, social and familial anxieties and stresses, real or perceived mistreatments and injustices at the hands of others, the desire for physical and intellectual gratifications of every sort, and the baser human emotions of vengeance, greed, envy, pride—that we inevitably lose focus on the God within, and lose sight of our innate moral compass. Communion with our Lord offers believers a way to refocus, to restore harmony with God."

Timothy's explanation was hitting home. "You said you could not prove your thesis logically, Timothy, yet I think I am persuaded!"

"Then the persuasion is through your heart rather than your head, Mark. But that is to be expected. Any quest for logical proof here is doomed to failure simply because the language of logic, like all language, grows out of our human experiences in the physical world. The experience of union with God must be expressed through metaphors and imagery, however imperfectly, because it transcends the concepts we are used to. Reasoning, ideas, and sensory images that grow out of the physical world and our emotional reactions to it are not useful here. The experience is more intuitive than logical. Perhaps a better word would be 'mystical.'"

"Define 'mystical.'"

"An awareness of God by direct experience rather than through logical reasoning. And, I contend, such direct experience of God is itself a gift, given most often, though not exclusively, to those who fervently seek Him."

"But there are many fervent seekers of God throughout the world, Timothy, of all religions. Can direct experience of union with God be theirs as well, wholly apart from knowledge of our Lord, or even of the Jewish scriptures?"

"Why should we discount that possibility? There are writings from the East, for example the Sanskrit poem *Song of God*, which speak directly to the nature of the soul and its relationship to God, teaching that with pure motives and virtuous lives, those who seek God as the ultimate goal of life will realize union with the divine. Are such writings not evidence of the universality of mystical experience?"

"I suppose so. But then, of what advantage is being a follower of Christ?"

"Much advantage in every way, Mark. Throughout history, religions have been created by man, evolving from the universal sentiments of awe, reverence and wonder at the immensity or mystery of the universe, and from speculations of the human mind seeking a way to explain them. Proponents of such religions may, in their fervor, become conscious of themselves as being in some relation with their god or gods, leading to some form of mystical experience. But all of the things we have spoken of at length—the incarnation of God-become-man, the perfect sacrifice for sin, the blessings of the Eucharistic meal, the communion of believers into one body—all are unique to the Christian believer, and all of them facilitate the experience of direct union. And besides," Timothy continued, "there is one more advantage that we have yet to discuss: the ultimate proof of the promise of eternal life, our Lord's resurrection from the dead."

I could hardly contain my excitement at the thought of piecing together Timothy's insights. "Let us discuss this now!" I insisted.

"I think, Mark, that tomorrow will be time enough to do so." With that, Timothy yawned and arose to stretch his legs, and motioned for me to do likewise. "Come, it is time now for prayer; let us give thanks for our safe passage this windy day, and welcome the evening."

The temperature was dropping with the sun, and Timothy sat and reached for Paul's cloak, draping half of it over his shoulders and motioning me to huddle next to him and share its warmth. As I went to sit beside him and join him in prayer, Timothy swung part of the cloak around me. Knowing that our sea voyage was ending, I could only hope that the land portion of our journey would offer equal opportunity for us to speak of these mysteries.

God, however, had other plans.

Chapter 10

I awoke to the rising sun as we completed our crossing, with the walled city of Brundisium shining in the eastern glow. As the first arrivals of the day, we easily made our way through the narrow straight that connected the protected harbor with the Adriatic, and headed for the first empty wharf, where there was room for all three boats in our convoy to tie up. Timothy and I secured our trunks for lowering to the dock, and waited our turn to go ashore.

As I stepped onto Italian soil for the first time in years, my apprehension suddenly grew. It would take perhaps a week along the Via Appia to reach Rome, but the great city somehow seemed palpably near. I thought of Paul, wondering how he was faring, hoping he was well.

Timothy left me with the trunks and immediately set out to hire a *raeda*, a four-wheeled coach with notched high sides and seats for a few passengers, drawn by oxen or mules. He returned with good news. "It is fortunate that we have arrived so early, Mark; we have a choice of *raedae* at reasonable prices, and I have found a sturdy one with two strong horses to bear us to Tarentum, before nightfall if we leave quickly." Spending the night in Tarentum, a good sized port city on the opposite side of the heel of Italy, was preferable to staying at one of the hostels in the countryside, which were more prone to be visited by brigands.

At length we boarded the coach and secured our trunks for the bumpy ride ahead, Timothy and I occupying the rear bench, the driver in front. With a yell and the crack of his whip the driver urged our two horses ahead, and we were off.

Timothy smiled at me, a smile I had come to recognize. He knew I was not about to let pass an opportunity to continue our discussion, no matter how uncomfortable the ride. "Shall we talk now of our Lord's resurrection, Timothy?"

"As you wish, Mark. Would you have us begin with its significance, or with the basis for our belief that this ultimate, transforming event indeed occurred? Or," Timothy said with a wink, "are you sufficiently secure in your faith such that there is no need to discuss the latter?"

Judging from his expression, Timothy seemed to know my answer before I mouthed my response: "Perhaps it would do no harm to hear from you why you have no doubt as to the truth of the resurrection."

Timothy's smile widened. "You mean, why do I believe the tradition we have been given: that three days after his burial Jesus' empty tomb was discovered by Mary of Magdalene, Mary the mother of James, and Salome, who went to Peter and the others to report what they had seen? Why do I believe the accounts of the apostles who swear that after his death they encountered our Lord in the flesh, and not as a vision?"

"Yes, if you would not mind."

"Not at all. But let me ask this. Paul's letter to the Corinthian church mentions Jesus' appearance to five hundred at once, many of whom were surely still alive when he wrote. Do you think it possible that so many of Jesus' followers could have been mistaken as to what they believed they were seeing and hearing when they testify that they saw and spoke with him?"

"I think it improbable, but not impossible. To put it in terms of what is logically possible, as you have earlier explained that concept: yes, I suppose it is logically possible that so many could have shared an identical vision of Jesus risen from the dead, and misinterpreted it as a physical encounter. Indeed, it is logically possible that only a few of his followers deluded the rest as to what they had seen, weaving the resurrection story into the form which, thirty-odd years later, now forms part of our tradition."

"Deluded, you say!" Timothy appeared thoroughly amused. "I think I can persuade you that there has been no such delusion."

"How?"

"What would be the motive behind such a conspiracy, Mark? None of these so-called 'weavers of the resurrection story' have used the persuasion of others for personal gain, for glory or for anything but a life of sacrifice, have they?"

"No, clearly not."

"And if one were setting out to delude another about the resurrection, would it not be natural to embellish the details of the story in such a way as to make them more persuasive?"

"Of course."

"Yet the opposite has been done here."

"What do you mean?"

"Tell me, Mark: is it not the case under Jewish law that the testimony of women, unless they are victims testifying as accusers against an accused, lacks the value needed to convict in court?"

"That is so."

"Then if the details of the resurrection story were a fabrication—if an empty tomb was never discovered—is it likely that the fabricators would recount a discovery of the empty tomb by women rather than by men?"

"I see your point. Still, perhaps the empty tomb these women found was not the same one in which Jesus was ultimately laid, and the women were simply mistaken, but they nevertheless convinced the others that it was indeed the actual tomb in which he was laid."

"Even if these women were mistaken as to the tomb's location, surely *someone* knew its true location. If they were followers of Jesus, would they not have checked on the women's story themselves? And if they were *not* followers of Jesus, would they not have come forth with the proof of Jesus' decomposing body once his disciples began setting Jerusalem abuzz with stories of his resurrection?"

"Again I see your point. But what of *my* point? This could have been a shared vision, rather than an actual physical encounter."

"Have you ever heard, Mark, of an apparition shared by so many?"

"In truth, no. But perhaps there were not so many as Paul reports. How could Paul know that the number was truly as large as five hundred?"

Timothy's smile widened. "Paul has consistently pressed his claim to authority and to apostleship as derived from the risen Christ having appeared to him. If that is his credential for authority, then with all of the disputes between him and the elders, would he have been so careless as to needlessly multiply the number of rival claimants to such authority?"

Even I had to smile at the thought of Paul allowing any potential in his passionate polemics for undercutting his own position.

"And let us go further; as we have each seen through many examples, those who claim that he appeared to them in the flesh thereupon reordered their lives accordingly, and were willing to sacrifice greatly, some even to die, for what they believed. Is it likely that a mere vision could have inspired such allegiance?"

"I suppose not."

"Can we agree, then, that mass hallucination is not a plausible explanation; and indeed, that no other explanation of the resurrection story is as plausible as its truth?"

"We can. Thank you for expounding on the subject."

"It is my pleasure. But it remains for us to understand the significance of this triumph over death. Shall we now explore this together?"

"I would like nothing more."

"Then let us start with an important distinction, that between mere resuscitation of a dead body, restoring it to its previous state of animation only to have it die again eventually; and resurrection, invigorating a new and incorruptible body which is forever transformed, never to suffer infirmity, illness or death again. Do you grasp the distinction?"

"I do."

"And what are infirmity, illness and death? Are they not a corruption of man's bodily existence?"

"Indeed."

"Which does the Torah teach: that such bodily corruption was ever man's natural state from the moment of his creation, or that corruption of the body arose afterward?"

"The latter. It is written that man was doomed to die only after he had disobeyed God's commandment not to consume the fruit of the tree of knowledge of good and evil."

"And do you understand this explanation of Adam's fall to be a reference to the sin of pride, which is to say, grasping for equality with God?"

"I do."

"What shall we say, then; that it was this sin of pride, of reaching for equality with God, which ushered physical corruptibility and death into the world?"

"So it would seem."

"We discussed earlier your objection to the concept of a melding of God and man in one person, and of the obstacle presented by the Jewish insistence on a fundamental distinction between Creator and creature, which leads not only to a concept of God's 'otherness' from man, but of their incompatibility by nature."

"I recall it."

"That incompatibility by nature was bound up in the notion of man's sinfulness, was it not?"

"It was."

"And would you agree that two things can be different, be 'other,' yet not be opposed to each other—and indeed, be in perfect harmony?"

"That is certainly possible."

"If man is in opposition to God by virtue of being envious of His Godhood and of reaching for equality with God, what would happen if that sin of pride, that envy, that overreaching were to end? Would not the opposition of God and man that has existed since Adam cease, even if the 'otherness' of God and man did not?"

"It would."

"Do you recall the letter Paul wrote to the believers at Philippi, where he described our Lord as having done the precise opposite of what Adam, allegorically, had done; that is, *not* counting equality with God as something to be grasped at, but rather emptying himself of such equality and humbling himself as a slave, to the point of death on a cross?"

"I do!"

"And as we have discussed, our Lord offered himself as the perfect sacrifice for sin; do you recall?"

"Of course."

"So then, if the sin of man ushered in the corruption of his physical body, and if a full expiation for that sin was accomplished by our Lord's death, would it not follow that his resurrection effected a restoration of the original physical nature of man?"

"Yes, that follows!"

"Here, then, we see the primary significance of Jesus' bodily resurrection as fulfilling God's original purpose for mankind. It is the very confirmation of his work to reverse the curse, to redeem humanity from sin. It is, in other words, the proof of the efficacy of the cross."

How logical things all seemed when Timothy expounded on them! Hearing his explanation harkened back memories of how Paul had often compared Jesus to Adam. I saw clearly, for the first time, that by his resurrection our Lord had, in effect, restored Eden. And if the cherubim stationed to guard its entrance with fiery swords had now been dismissed, there could be no more important spiritual journey than the path back to those garden gates.

Timothy, however, was not finished. "Soon after we left Ephesus, Mark, when we began discussing eternal life, we agreed that it is not illogical for the soul to survive the body and enjoy eternal life because the soul is spirit, not flesh, and thus need not be affected by the corruption which overtakes our physical nature; do you recall?"

"I do."

"Well, if that physical nature were likewise not affected by corruption—if our bodies could be restored to the original physical nature they enjoyed before sin entered the world—would it not be possible to conclude that eternal life can await *both* body and soul?"

"It would."

"And if, after his death, our Lord's resurrection evidences such a restoration to the original physical nature of man, can not we who are granted salvation through our faith in him also expect the same resurrection, the same restoration—just as Paul wrote to the saints at Philippi?"

"I suppose so."

"Then our Lord's resurrection was but the precursor of our own; the resurrection of the body after death is what we have to look forward to as well. And here, we have a second significance of the resurrection: to show us what is possible, what awaits those who are saved from eternal death."

"But if Paul is right that flesh and blood cannot inherit the kingdom of God, that we must be transformed, what can such a risen body be like? Is it identical to ours in every way except that it is imperishable? Does it feel pleasure and pain, hunger and thirst?"

"Well, it has been reported that the disciples saw our Lord eat and drink after his resurrection. Whether he only seemed to do so, as the Book of Tobit reports of the angel Raphael, I cannot say. Perhaps as an angel's body differs from a human's, so shall it be for us. The precise characteristics of this risen body, I am afraid, I cannot describe. I have never examined an angel up close!"

"But if our physical bodies are to occupy it, must not heaven then be a place of spatial dimension, a physical location somewhere in the universe?"

"Do you recall our discussion of the soul being free of both temporal and physical dimensions, Mark? If such a soul is to be conjoined to a resurrected body, then heaven must be a 'place' unlike one we are used to if it is to be eternal in the sense we discussed earlier—timeless, changeless. For example, it must be a place where the sun does not rise and set, lest a measure of change, and therefore of time, be introduced. Still, I would think that the physical experience of its residents must be somewhat akin to that of beings who inhabit a true space with height, depth and width—for if it were otherwise, the resurrection of the body would hardly be recognizable as such, would it?"

"I agree. But wherever heaven is, how are our physical bodies to get there once resurrected? Is heaven a distant place on the earth, akin to Plato's mythical island of Atlantis? Does it lie beyond the stars?"

"If I could point out the ship of transport to the Elysian fields, I would truly be the most blessed of men! No, Mark, there are some things we must take on faith, and content ourselves with the promise of eternal life in whatever form of new world God has prepared for us. But this much can be said: the truth of our Lord's bodily resurrection and his ultimate ascension to the Father—perhaps I should say his physical 'relocation' rather than 'ascension' so as not to imply that the direction of heaven is 'up'—can only bode well for those who experience union with him. And as I hold to that truth, I am confident that just as our experience of union with God here on earth is as bodily *persons*, not as ghosts, so shall it be in the hereafter."

Satisfied with his explanation, Timothy turned away and gazed in silence at the passing countryside, clothed in olive trees and vineyards, as we bounced along the road. It was clear that he was tiring, and had had enough discussion for now. I did not press him further. Timothy was right in what he had said at the beginning of our journey: if logical proof were available for every proposition, there would hardly be room for faith.

As evening descended our driver announced that we were entering Tarentum, and that he would be dropping us at his uncle's inn, "the most comfortable in the city, and a bargain as well!" His salesmanship was hardly needed; Timothy and I were worn out from nearly twelve hours of bumpy ride at a quick pace, and in no mood to search for lodging.

The inn that we arrived at was modest but welcoming, and appeared reasonably clean. With his nephew's introduction the proprietor greeted us, and after a quick negotiation on price we were directed to a room in the rear, where we deposited our trunks. Hungry for something to eat, I left Timothy there to rest, and made my way to the inn's great room.

By the light of a single lamp, perhaps a dozen men were gathered in conversation. As I approached, I could see that the men were listening intently to a balding, grey figure with his broad back to me, speaking in Greek but with the distinctive Aramaic accent so familiar to me from my youth. I gasped audibly as I heard his words:

". . . and attest through my own witness that Jesus of Nazareth lives on, and continues to work great miracles to this very day . . ."

The old man turned around as he heard my gasp, and our eyes met. I knew those eyes well.

It was Peter!

Chapter 11

In our dimly lit back room Peter, Timothy and I, our shock beginning to wear off, huddled together to pray and to exchange news of our trips. Peter told us of how his ship had left Joppa nearly a month ago, bound for Ostia, the port of Rome, but had been blown off course into the Bay of Tarentum by a sudden storm from the southwest. He was traveling alone, and had been staying here at the inn for three days already, called by the Spirit to delay his journey in order to preach in Tarentum for a time. "The storm was not fortuitous, my brothers; the citizens here are hungry for the gospel."

"It is truly a blessing for us that you are headed to Rome, Peter; but what is your purpose there?" I asked. "Is it to speak with Paul?" It was common knowledge that ever since Paul's public insult to Peter in Antioch years earlier, accusing him of hypocrisy for at first deigning and later refusing to share a table with the Gentiles there, the two had not communicated—and ever since then I had secretly been praying that one day they would reconcile their differences.

"Not primarily," Peter replied, "although I do think it is high time to try to heal the rift between us. I will surely speak with him, and attempt to convince him that his work in Rome and mine are not in conflict. My purpose there is simply to encourage and strengthen the Roman church, to the end that it may gain a position of prominence in the world. Rome is the crossroads of the empire; what better place to serve as the base of the Faith?"

To hear a Jew refer to any city other than Jerusalem as the center of faith was quite remarkable, and Peter must have seen the look of puzzlement on my face. "Looking back now, Mark, I see how predictable this shift was. In no small measure due to Paul's work, the gospel has gained great acceptance with Gentiles throughout the empire, and as it has, the Temple in Jerusalem has become less and less the center of the Faith. I no longer feel that the Temple must serve as a focal point." Peter's voice suddenly lowered. "Indeed, I am not sure that it will survive to serve that function much longer."

"What do you mean, Peter?"

"Relations in Jerusalem between the zealots and the Roman legions grow ever more tense, and now that Gessius Florus has been appointed as the new Procurator things are bound to get even worse. I suspect that there will be armed conflict one day, conflict which may lead to the destruction of the Temple—just as our Lord predicted."

"I fear that things are not much better for the believers in Rome than they are for Jews in Jerusalem," Timothy said, and produced the letter he had received from Paul. He allowed Peter to read it in full before speaking further. "I think," Timothy said when Peter had finished reading, "Paul has need of much more than his cloak. Does not his letter have the tone of one who is realizing he has come near to the end of his mission?"

There was an expression of concern on Peter's weathered face. "I agree. You were right to embark quickly. There will be a time of trial ahead for the church in Rome, and we must do all we can to strengthen the believers there in the face of the Emperor's mounting instability. Tomorrow morning, Timothy, you must leave for Rome. But leave Mark here with me a while longer, as I have need of him in finishing the work of the Spirit here. We will join you in Rome soon enough."

I glanced at Timothy, who made no protest to this suggestion—perhaps because he acknowledged Peter's authority to countermand Paul's directive, more likely because he was simply too exhausted to argue the point. The discussion we had had soon after leaving Ephesus of Peter's primacy in matters of doctrine received from the Lord was one thing. But my itinerary was not a doctrinal matter, and Timothy had spent his entire adult life as the close disciple and friend of the man whose explicit instructions he had set out to follow, instructions that Peter had just altered.

"I will stay on in Tarentum a while longer, then," I said. "Timothy can bring the parchments up to Paul ahead of us."

"No," Peter replied. "Leave the parchments with us, Timothy. It will be safer for them to travel in the company of two men rather than one." The logic of that request must have satisfied Timothy, as he immediately retrieved the parchments and handed them to me.

Peter and I let Timothy retire and went back to the inn's great room to talk further for a while. Despite my exhaustion, I was anxious to question Peter about his shift in focus away from the Temple and toward Rome, and to find out whether this meant he had come around more to Paul's way of thinking, or was planning a challenge to Paul's preaching. But Peter quickly dispelled my concerns.

"Do not trouble yourself, Mark. Whatever our differences, Paul and I share one service of Christ. There is room in that service for more than one approach. I trust that Paul would not condemn those of us who preach that Jewish believers should continue to observe the Sabbath, the Jewish festivals, dietary rules and circumcision. Neither do I condemn him for preaching that Gentile believers are free from such observance."

"Did Jesus ever indicate which view *he* favored?"

"As a Jew in the midst of Jews, he had no occasion to minister to Gentiles, so it is impossible to know; but among Jews at least, his approach was mixed. In some respects his observance of the Law was relaxed, particularly in his willingness to have contact with those who were ritually impure for one reason or another, and his insistence that foods thought to be impure could not defile a person. But he never abandoned the core of Judaism. I can think of one very clear example. Hand me the parchments, Mark," Peter instructed. I did so, and he spread them before us. "See here:

> 'A man asked him, "Which is the first of all the commandments?" Jesus answered, "This is the first: 'Hear, O Israel! The Lord our God is One! Therefore you shall love the Lord your God with all your heart, with all your soul, with all your strength.' And this is the second: 'You shall love your neighbor as yourself.' There is no commandment greater than these."'

Would Jesus have recited the *Shema* as part of his instruction if he had not intended his listeners to maintain the basic religious traditions of Judaism?"

"Your point is well taken, Peter—but as you say, Jesus was addressing Jews, not Gentiles. Do you say Paul is in error for teaching that Gentiles need not adopt Jewish traditions?"

"I say no such thing. It is better to focus on our common message than to dwell on our disparate interpretations, for in the end, most of our differences are not on vital matters. It has taken me some time to realize this; and if only Paul were less headstrong, perhaps he would realize it as well."

"Headstrong he is, Peter, but a tireless champion of the Way. May I live to see the day when the two of you embrace!"

"Pray, then, that Paul has become less vitriolic over the years." My expression must have given away my surprise at this statement. "Yes, Mark, I have read what he wrote to the Galatians about my dinner arrangements in Antioch!"

Peter's countenance took on an air of genuine sadness as he continued. "Paul, James and I had all agreed back in Jerusalem that Paul's mission would be to the Gentiles, mine to the Jews—and if I erred at all in Antioch, it was in joining in table fellowship with Paul's group in the first place. I should have foreseen that Paul would view such table fellowship as my complete rejection of the Law, and spin it to his own advantage. When James' contingent came up from Jerusalem and pointed out that I was becoming a source of scandal to the very group I had been commissioned with reaching, I knew they were right. So did we all, even your cousin Barnabas. Paul protested. But in the end it was Paul alone, not I, who was obliged to leave Antioch, castigated for his outbursts. Yet his letter never mentions that fact; instead, he portrays the events as though *he* were the victor in some decisive battle over the Faith. In truth, I would not have been surprised to read that I had *conceded* my mistake, and immediately resumed eating with the Gentiles! Doubtless I have escaped *that* fabrication only through Paul's concern that there may have been eyewitnesses among the Galatians reading his letter."

Peter's account was the same as I had heard from Barnabas, who had vowed never again to accompany Paul on another mission, so strongly did he feel that Paul was in the wrong. Peter, however, clearly held no similar grudge.

"Your forgiveness of Paul is commendable, Peter."

Peter sighed deeply. "How could I *not* forgive him? As you say, he is a tireless champion of the Way, although his path is not always the same as mine, and I sometimes wonder if Paul is not following *his* way rather than *the* Way. To the Galatians he has characterized the Law as impossible to obey completely, and therefore as the curse of death—ignoring all of the prophets who preached that repentance leads to forgiveness! What Jew would ever say such a thing? Still, Paul has convinced many in Galatia to embrace the gospel, and for that reason I suppose I should give thanks to God if it suited his purposes with the Galatians to paint me as the fool."

"Paint you the fool? What need could Paul have had in doing so?"

"In order to stress to the Galatians that observance of the Law does not lead to justification before God. His overriding concern was that they should resist the Judaizers, lest they place their faith in ritual observances rather than in God alone. With that concern, I agree; requiring such observances of Gentiles is pointless, for doing so cannot justify them. But neither is there harm in continued observance of the Law, by Jews *and* Gentiles, so long as both groups accept that their justification is likewise by faith. To say, as Paul did to the Galatians, that the Law was valid only until Christ came is to misunderstand its value. There is much in the Law which is good, and which profits one to follow."

After years of hearing Paul's teachings on this subject, I was anxious to explore Peter's views, to see how they might differ. "Tell me, then. What portions of the Law remain of advantage, and how are we to know which precepts should be followed and which may be safely ignored?"

"True morality and right conduct we know innately, and that innate moral sense provides the distinction you seek." Peter was beginning to sound a bit like Timothy. "Does not Paul teach, for example, that dietary restrictions are not binding, but sexual licentiousness must be shunned? Why, if both are part of the Law? Has Paul picked and chosen at random? No, Mark. Even though the Law makes no distinction between rules of expediency and rules of ethics, we ourselves know the difference. As Jeremiah said, with the coming of the new covenant the law is written not in any text, but in our hearts.

"It is the heart that is the repository of good or of evil in a person, and the intention in one's heart will determine the benefit of keeping a ritual of the Law. Jesus once said that nothing which enters a man from outside can defile him, for such things as enter the stomach and pass into the latrine do not remain in the heart. Rather, the evil intentions which come out of a man's heart—fornication, theft, murder, adultery, greed, malice, deceit, envy, slander, pride—these are the things that defile."

This was sounding very much like what Paul preached. "And if we follow our hearts, Peter, is there any further profit in observance of the Law for we who are Jews, yet believe in Christ as the path to salvation?"

"Faith in Christ sets us on that path, but we must also journey along that path in righteousness. And here, the Law retains some merit. Leaving ritual cleanliness, sacrifices and feast observances aside, the Law and the Prophets contain many precepts which are guideposts to the moral life, and contain commandments for avoidance of sin and evil. If we ignore these precepts we do so at our peril, for God's justice will be served, and our faith will not save us if we do not put it into practice by leading the moral life."

"Yet Paul stresses faith, and not works, as the exclusive means to justification before God."

"And so he should, Mark; but take care that you do not confuse justification with sanctification. Justification—which is to say, forgiveness of our sins and consequent righteousness before God—is brought about by faith in the sacrifice of our Savior Jesus Christ; it is this which satisfies the demands of God's justice in the face of our sins and reconciles us to God. Sanctification—which is to say, the active process of the believer's chosen life of holiness—is brought about by choosing to behave morally, to avoid sin and to demonstrate through our actions a love of God and our neighbor. Both are a matter of God's grace. And both are necessary to salvation. Those who seek salvation by the sincere performance of good works alone are doomed to failure, if they have not been first justified by faith. Likewise, those who rely solely on their justification through faith for their salvation, but thereafter do not live according to the Spirit they have received, also are doomed to failure."

"But does not one flow naturally from the other?" I asked. "Is not justification through faith in Christ a guarantee of sanctification as well?"

"You ask two different questions, Mark! Yes, the same faith which justifies may also lead one to be sanctified, by implanting in the believer the will to act in accordance with God's will. But that is not a necessary consequence. Free choice remains to be exercised. A person chooses to *believe*, and also chooses to *behave*—and one can make the first choice yet not make the second in harmony with the first."

"But if a man truly believes something, surely he will act in accordance with that belief." Now it was I who was beginning to sound like Timothy. "If one behaves other than in accordance with one's professed belief, does that not betray the belief as not truly held to begin with?"

"You confuse faith with faithfulness, Mark. We do not cast off human flaws and weaknesses simply by believing in the saving gospel of Jesus of Nazareth. By that faith the slate is instantly wiped clean—and handed back to us. How we will write on it after that is up to each of us, with all our flaws and frailties, but also with the saving grace of God to help us overcome them."

"You are saying, then, that one's faith alone does not necessarily ensure ultimate salvation," I replied. "I am not sure Paul would agree."

"Oh? Did his letter not sternly warn the Galatians that fornication, licentiousness, idolatry, enmity, anger, selfishness, envy and the like must be avoided by all those who would inherit the kingdom of God? Yet he was writing to *believers*, to those who had *already* been justified by their faith! What point would there have been to such warnings if the sanctification of the believers were automatic? No, Mark. Paul understands well that faith is neither a license to sin, nor a guarantee that sin will be avoided—and a sinful life will bring God's harsh judgment on the sinner, believer and nonbeliever alike."

"Yet Paul also proclaims that having been justified and reconciled to God by our Lord's death, much more so shall we be saved by his life."

"And so we shall—*if* we allow his life to guide our own. You must recognize that Paul is a skilled rhetorician, who sometimes chooses to express himself in the language of certainty so as to encourage his audience. But take it from a poor fisherman: we must work out our own salvation by living in accordance with God's will, avoiding temptations, confessing and repenting of our sins when we fall. If we have the will to do so, then by the saving grace of God we shall have the power also."

Clearly this was no poor fisherman sitting before me. To look into Peter's face was to look into the very face of certainty. His words resonated with authority and truth.

We shared a brief prayer and said our good nights, and I returned to my room with Peter's admonition about the necessity of leading a moral life ringing in my head. Without waking Timothy I spread the parchments on top of my trunk, and in the dim light of my waning candle, I quickly found the passage I sought:

> *'If your hand is your difficulty, cut it off: it is better to enter into life maimed, than to have two hands and enter into Gehenna, with its fire that never shall be quenched. And if your foot is your undoing, cut it off: it is better to enter into life crippled, than to have two feet and be cast into hell. And if your eye is your downfall, pluck it out: it is better to enter into the kingdom of God with one eye, than to be cast with both eyes into Gehenna, where the worm dies not, and the fire is not quenched.'*

And I prayed fervently as my candle burnt down and finally out.

Chapter 12

Soon after sunrise, before the others had awakened, I ventured out into the still Tarentine air to walk for a while through the city. An event reminiscent of Passover had occurred in these very streets nearly three centuries earlier. During the Second Punic War, Tarentum was sympathetic to Carthage and aided Hannibal in overthrowing Roman occupation of the city. On the night of his surprise attack against the Roman cohorts, Hannibal had ensured that his soldiers would respect the locals' property by arranging for the Tarentines to mark their houses with chalk so that only those not so marked, and thus belonging to Romans, were sacked.

Peter had said he wanted my help, and I was anxious to learn precisely how. I knew Peter did not speak Latin well, which was not a serious problem in Tarentum but could present difficulties as we approached Rome. Did he need me in order to translate for him? Or did he have a greater purpose in mind? I would not have long to wait for my answer.

On returning to the inn I found Peter and Timothy awake, the younger man packing for imminent departure. We embraced, and Timothy smiled at me and then at Peter. "I will see you both in Rome, and let Paul and the others know that you will be coming soon. Mark, take care not to let Peter exert himself unduly; despite his broad shoulders, he is not as young as he likes to think! Blessings on you both for a speedy and safe journey."

"And on you," Peter replied. "Go with Christ, and our love." We helped Timothy load his trunk onto his waiting wagon, embraced him once again, and then he was off, waving back to us as he faded into the distance.

After a quick prayer for Timothy's wellbeing, Peter informed me that he had been invited to speak at the local synagogue. It was the Sabbath, and Tarentum had a substantial Jewish population, many of them recent converts to Judaism. Peter hoped for a large turnout.

When we arrived, we were greeted by some of the men with whom Peter had been speaking at the inn the night before. After donning a tallis and reciting the *berachah*, Peter turned to me and asked, "Mark, would you be willing to say a few words about the Way? I have need of a witness." I agreed without hesitation—or at least, I hoped, without visible hesitation. "Excellent! Then come up and stand by my side when I read from Torah."

When the prayers and singing of the psalms had concluded and it was Peter's time to read and address the congregation, we made our way to the bimah. Peter took the scroll and began to read from the Book of Numbers:

> *'These were the dedication offering for the altar from the leaders of Israel when it was anointed: twelve silver dishes, twelve silver bowls, twelve gold pans, each silver dish weighing one hundred and thirty shekels and each bowl seventy; so that all the silver of these vessels came to two thousand four hundred shekels, according to the standard of the sanctuary; and the twelve gold pans, full of incense, weighed ten shekels apiece, according to the standard of the sanctuary, so that all the gold of the pans weighed one hundred twenty shekels. The animals for the burnt offering were as follows: twelve young bulls, and twelve yearling lambs with their grain offering, and twelve male goats for a sin offering; and for the sacrifice of peace offerings twenty four oxen, sixty rams, sixty male goats, and sixty yearling lambs. These were the dedication offering for the altar after it was anointed.'*

When he had finished, he addressed his audience in Greek, with the confidence and conviction that was his hallmark:

"Citizens of Tarentum, thank you for this chance to speak. I have lately come from Jerusalem, from worship at the Temple. The sight of its grandeur, which some of you have seen, is inspiring. The sweet smell of incense, and the pungent odor of the burnt animal fat of the sacrificial offerings, remains in my nostrils even now. Being present at the Temple sacrifice is a moving experience for any Jew.

"Yet we read in the Psalms,

> 'You do not delight in sacrifices, if I should offer it; you do not take pleasure in burnt offerings. My sacrifice, O God, is a contrite spirit; a broken and contrite heart, O God, you will not spurn.'

So do we read in the first Book of Samuel,

> 'Does the Lord so delight in burnt offerings and sacrifices, as in obeying the commandments of the Lord? Behold, obedience is better than sacrifice, and submission than the fat of rams.'

Even has the prophet Micah written:

> 'With what shall I come before the Lord and bow down before the exalted God? Shall I come before him with burnt offerings, with calves a year old? Will the Lord be pleased with thousands of rams, with ten thousand rivers of oil? He has showed you, O man, what is good, and what the Lord requires of you. Only to do justice, and to love mercy and to walk humbly with your God.'

And also the prophet Hosea:

> 'For I desire love, not sacrifice, and knowledge of God rather than burnt offerings.'

"What is it, then, that entices God to forgive our sins? Is it the sacrifice on His altar, or is it the repentance of a contrite heart? In truth, I am persuaded that it is both; one has no efficacy without the other. Thus, after the dedication of the Temple altar, it is written that the Lord appeared to Solomon and said

> 'I have heard your prayer, and I have chosen this place for my house of sacrifice.'

—but immediately also

> 'If my people, who are called by my name, shall humble themselves, and pray, and seek my face, and turn from their evil ways; then will I hear from heaven, and will forgive their sin, and will heal their land.'

"Yes, my friends, God's forgiveness requires that we turn from wickedness and obey Him. Without this, all sacrifices come to naught.

"When I was a young man in Galilee and curious about these mysteries, I and many others went out to the desert to hear John the Baptiser, who proclaimed a baptism of repentance which led to the forgiveness of sins. No doubt many of you have heard of him. Hundreds were baptized by him in the river Jordan, vowing to reform their lives. Yet his message was always thus: 'One more powerful than I is yet to come, and I am not fit to stoop and untie his sandals. I have baptized you in water; but he will baptize you in the Holy Spirit.' I pondered who this other might be, and what this Holy Spirit was.

"By the grace of God, I have found both answers. You have all heard about Jesus of Nazareth, and of the many miracles he performed throughout Judea. He appeared in Galilee soon after John the Baptiser, likewise preaching that the reign of God was at hand, and urging all who would listen to reform their lives and believe in the gospel he preached, a gospel which I was blessed to hear personally. That gospel is simply this: if we love God and one another as we love ourselves, and place our faith in God's saving grace through a sacrifice born of obedience to the law of love that undergirds the Law of Moses, the spirit of God shall be ours on this earth, and eternal life in the world to come.

"Jesus both preached and lived obedience to the law of love, and was the very embodiment of his message. His crucifixion at the hands of the Roman authorities on the insistence of the chief priest and scribes whose authority he challenged is well known, as are the reports of his resurrection from the dead, which seems so incredible to many. Yet I vouch to you, it is no rumor; I myself saw him, in the flesh, risen from the dead! After his resurrection I ate and drank with him, walked with him, talked with him. My testimony is true, and confirmed by many others. It was impossible for death to hold him, in such measure as he had the spirit of God. In obedience to the law of love he himself was sacrificed for our sins, a sacrifice compared to which all the burnt offerings offered at the Temple altar pale. He is the Messiah foretold of old, not as a king by earthly measure, but as one ushering in the heavenly reign of God.

"That reign is upon us, my friends. The sacrifice it requires of us is not of goats or rams, nor of rituals and feast observances, but of love of all mankind, even our enemies, and of faithfulness to the belief in the saving power of Jesus Christ. On those who believe this gospel with their whole heart, the power of the Holy Spirit will descend, to strengthen and ultimately to save when Jesus Christ returns again in glory as he promised. I am witness to the saving power of the Holy Spirit, in my own life and in the lives of many believers. There are many others as well."

Peter nodded to me, as the required second witness readily at hand. I stepped forward and added my corroboration: "What Peter says is true. I too have seen the power of the Holy Spirit, in my own life and in the lives of other believers."

At that point we were peppered with questions, all of which Peter answered with aplomb, meeting the arguments of even the skeptics calmly, yet with authority. His charisma was as undeniable as his humility.

It soon became clear that we had found fertile ground in which to sow the seed of the Way. As was true throughout the Diaspora, a good number of those in the congregation were dissatisfied with the slavish practice of ritual by which they had defined themselves up to now, and were sympathetic to Peter's message. Moreover, here on the Italian peninsula, none were zealots seeking a Messiah who would overthrow Roman rule.

"What shall we do, then?" some of them began to ask each other. Peter quickly responded, "Commit to reform your lives, place your faith in the gospel you have heard, and be baptized in the name of God, of Jesus Christ and of the Holy Spirit. Any of you who would do so, come with me now; not to the *mikveh* where the proselyte is immersed upon coming to Torah, but down to the bay. You will be baptized this very hour!"

The first to press through the congregation and come up to Peter and myself was an old man with a hunched back. "My name is Amasianus," he said loudly as he bowed even more deeply before us. "I am caretaker for the Mayor, tending his gardens on the shores of the bay. I hear in your voice the voice of God, and believe the truth of your words. I would be baptized."

"Praise be to God for the faith of this man!" Peter exclaimed as he placed his hand on the hunchback's shoulder. "Come, then, let us go down to the bay." With that, Peter turned and left the Temple, with Amasianus and myself close behind, and the entire congregation in tow. As we headed down through the narrow streets of the city, our chattering parade grew even larger, drawing the curious to follow.

Within a few minutes we arrived at the water's edge. Hundreds were now gathered on the shore, shoulder to shoulder, many of them straining for an unobstructed view, as Peter led Amasianus out into the water until it reached his chest. Peter then clasped his left hand on the hunchback's arm, placed his right on top of his head, and pushed his head under the water three times, crying out: "Be thou baptized and consecrated to God in the name of Jesus Christ!"

I was not the first to notice it as the two men waded back to shore, but the gasps of astonishment and bulging eyes of the onlookers focused my attention at once on Amasianus—and as I beheld him, all of the breath I could hold rushed into my lungs as well.

The curvature had completely left his spine; he stood erect and straight!

Chapter 13

The ensuing three days were a whirlwind of activity. Not only were many of the onlookers from the synagogue also baptized, but as word of Amasianus' miraculous cure spread quickly throughout Tarentum, Jews and Gentiles alike sought out Peter and me, and many of them were baptized as well. Our time was almost unceasingly spent in preaching the Way, instructing the new believers in the faith—and as I learned from Peter, so was I able to impart much to my own listeners. Hundreds of believers were added, including even the Mayor of the city and his family.

Amasianus himself became our inseparable companion, and as he learned more of the Way, anyone could see in him the deepest conviction. The boldness he had shown in stepping forward at the synagogue was equally evident in his enthusiasm for spreading the message of what God had done for him. "After we leave for Rome," Peter predicted, "he will become the leader of the church here."

Listening to Peter talk to the Tarentines about Jesus rekindled the excitement I had felt in my youth when I first heard Peter speak. Unlike Timothy, who persuaded by calm logic, Peter simply exuded charisma. There was no man I admired more. I was looking forward to having him to myself for the time it would take us to reach Rome, so much so that even my apprehension over what would occur when we arrived there was gone.

As was the custom in new churches, charity among the believers ruled their relations. Hostilities were forgotten, replaced with communal prayer and thanksgiving. Whether of noble or peasant birth, whether slave or free, whether male or female, they treated each other as equals, broke bread and prayed together, sharing their possessions with those less well off. The Mayor himself insisted on giving Peter and me one of his own horses and a cart to bear us to Rome, which we gratefully accepted.

On the morning we were to leave, a crowd of believers gathered to see us off. In front of all of them, Peter laid his hands on Amasianus' head, this time not to immerse him but to commission him. "Continue to preach with conviction what you have heard from us, remain steadfast and encourage the others in prayer and in charity. Give thanks for what God has done for you, and serve him by doing for others as much as you are able. In all things, conduct yourself as a model citizen of heaven so that others, in seeing your faith, will persevere all the more in their own. Baptize those who commit to the faith just as you were baptized. Share the bread and wine in commemoration of our Lord's sacrifice just as you have seen us do. Welcome those from other churches as they pass this way. Have no fear of any man, nor of any earthly thing, but let the spirit of the Lord guide you in all things. God willing, we will return this way again."

"Amen," Amasianus responded. The three of us embraced warmly, after which Amasianus insisted on loading our trunks in the back of the cart himself. "My back is strong," he said with a broad smile.

"Of that I am certain, my brother!" Peter replied.

We climbed atop the cart, and as I took the reins to urge our horse on, Peter gave the crowd a final blessing. "The grace and peace of the Lord be with you and remain with you, my friends!" And to cries of "*Vale*" and "Go with God," we left the crowd of converts and headed toward Silvium, the next substantial city along the Appian Way.

"Tell me, Peter," I asked at length, "Did you know in advance that Amasianus would be cured at his baptism?"

"I suspected it. His faith was clearly genuine, and I have often seen such miracles occur in the presence of genuine faith. The power of God seems naturally to descend on a person in proportion to one's response to His call. God was calling Amasianus, and he responded."

"And what of your own calling, Peter; how did it come about?"

Peter's eyes twinkled a bit, and his lips curled into a slight smile. "I was a young man of twenty-one, recently married, living in Capernaum on the northwest shore of the Sea of Galilee. Although I had heard about Jesus' preaching from others, I never went to seek him out as I had John the Baptizer. He found *me*. Late one afternoon I was fishing with my brother Andrew, and from our boat not far off shore I suddenly saw him standing at the water's edge. He had a certain aura about him, almost a glow—a captivating presence apparent even at a distance. As our gazes met, he called out to us to come ashore. And so we did. As we were beaching the boat, he simply said 'Come follow me; I will make you fishers of men.'"

"Did you do so at once?"

"Without any hesitation whatsoever. In that moment no explanation was needed; somehow we just knew that it was the right thing to do. We left the boat and the nets there on the shore, and followed him—without asking a single question of who he was, where he was leading us, or even what he meant by 'fishers of men.' As strange as it sounds, we simply trusted him. And we were not alone. A little farther up the shoreline, Jesus called out to two friends of mine, James and John, the sons of Zebedee, who were also in their boat with their father and some others, working their nets. James and John did precisely as Andrew and I had done; they dropped everything and immediately followed him. It was that way as well with Levi the tax collector, son of Alphaeus; a simple 'Follow me' from Jesus, and he left his post and followed. It was that way with all twelve of us who followed him. Jesus' words simply held that authority. And not only over men."

"Over what else?"

"To begin with, over the elements. Have I never told you about the miracle he performed in calming a tempest on the Sea of Galilee, when our boat was about to founder? He was sleeping peacefully in the stern, oblivious to the storm. When we woke him, he simply commanded the storm 'Be still!'—and at once the wind and waves obeyed him. Not since Moses parted the Red Sea had any man wielded the power of God in such a way. And another time, when we were out on the lake without him before dawn and being tossed violently by the wind, he came walking on the water toward us, got in the boat, and calmed the wind! Neither the forces of nature, nor even the forces of Satan, could resist his word."

"The forces of Satan as well?"

"Indeed. The very first day after he called us, it was the Sabbath, and Jesus was preaching in the synagogue in Capernaum. He spoke with the authority of a prophet, unlike the rabbis and scribes we were used to. Suddenly a man possessed of a demon came running into the synagogue, shrieking at Jesus 'What do you want of us, Jesus of Nazareth? Have you come to destroy us? I know who you are, the holy one of God!' We were all stunned into silence; but Jesus commanded the demon, 'Be still! Leave this man!' At once the man went into convulsions, and the unclean spirit left him with a loud scream that faded somewhere, invisibly, within the walls of the synagogue—until all was quiet again! We all looked at each other in amazement, asking ourselves what this could mean, what manner of man this Jesus could be, whose words had authority not only in preaching, but even over demonic spirits!

"In any event, you can well imagine the stir that this exorcism caused in the synagogue. Before word of it could spread through the town, Andrew, James, John and I quickly escorted Jesus to my house. But escape from the crowds was futile; they soon found us there. This day was to be a day of miracles."

"What else happened that day?"

"First, my mother-in-law was in bed with fever; he promptly healed her simply by taking her hand and helping her up. Then, when the Sabbath had ended, many townspeople began coming to the house, and throughout the evening he proceeded to heal them from illnesses of various kinds, and from demons.

"I am sure this would have gone on for many days had he not left the house before we awoke the next morning. When we tracked him down in the desert later that day, he bade us follow him to the other villages of Galilee, saying 'I must proclaim the good news there as well; that is what I have come to do.' And so we went with him to the neighboring towns, where he preached in their synagogues as well, and cured many.

"A few days later we returned to Capernaum, and when the news of our arrival got out, the throngs lined up at my house were even greater than before. One could hardly get near my front door, so thick were the crowds hoping to see Jesus and be healed by him. A group of four men bearing a paralytic on his pallet were especially enterprising; they scampered onto the roof, cut a hole through the reeds and mud thatch, and lowered the paralyzed man on his mat between the rafters. Jesus was clearly moved by their faith in him. But when he said to the paralytic 'My son, your sins are forgiven,' it caused quite a stir."

"How so?"

"There were some scribes in the room who took affront to this statement, no doubt judging it blasphemous. As if he knew their thoughts, Jesus looked at them with that piercing stare of his, and answered them: 'Which is easier: to say "Your sins are forgiven," or "Stand up, pick up your mat, and walk?" But in order that you may know that I have been given authority on earth to forgive sins'—and at that, he turned to the paralytic and said, 'Stand up! Pick up your pallet and go!' At once the man stood and picked up his mat, and left the house to the amazement of us all—even the scribes!"

Although it must have been obvious to all present that they were witnessing a true mircale, I could not help but feel some sympathy for the scribes' dilemma. This was not a case of a prophet simply declaring that *God* had forgiven a man's sins, as the prophet Nathan had declared to David after he had arranged the death of Uriah the Hittite. Here was Jesus saying that *he himself* had been given such authority. Under the Law, not only was it God's exclusive province to forgive sins, but forgiveness came only through the prescribed sacrifice in the Temple—and from all appearances, none had been offered. What were the scribes to think? Instant reassessment of a lifetime of learning on the subject could not have come easily to them. "And did the scribes then come to believe in him as well?" I inquired.

"Far from it; they felt provoked, and set out to trap him. In retrospect, I believe he was deliberately provoking them. Not long afterwards, when he was preaching again in the synagogue on the Sabbath, a man with a shriveled hand was present. Jesus called him up front, and then asked the scribes 'Is it permitted to do a good deed on the Sabbath?' When they did not answer, he turned to the man and said 'Stretch out your hand.' As soon as the man did so, his hand was perfectly restored! But even this did not convince the scribes to follow him. Indeed, I think this was the beginning of their plotting against him.

"There were other skirmishes with the scribes and Pharisees over what was or was not permitted behavior. Once, when they observed us eating without washing our hands first, they asked Jesus 'Why do your disciples not follow the tradition of our ancestors and wash their hands before taking food?' Knowing that the Torah included no such command, Jesus answered by quoting from Isaiah, *'This people pays me lip service but their hearts are far from me. In vain is their worship of me, the rote observance of merely human precepts.'* The scribes and Pharisees were outraged by this.

"Their anger grew in proportion to his fame. People were coming to Galilee from everywhere—Judea, Jerusalem, Idumea, the Transjordan, even the regions around Tyre and Sidon. The healings and exorcisms continued. Wherever he made an appearance, in any village or at any crossroads, people laid the sick out in the marketplaces and begged him to let them touch just a tassel of his robe."

Those tassels, I thought to myself, could only mean one thing: *Jesus was a Torah-observant Jew*. Intentionally or not, Peter was painting a picture of Jesus quite different from that painted by Paul, whose pre-conversion persecution of the first Christians out of "zeal for the law" had always suggested to me that Jesus and his followers must have been anything but Torah-observant.

"Soon," Peter continued, "the press of humanity was so great that we had to retreat into a fishing boat on the lake, and after that, to a mountain top. It was there that Jesus appointed twelve from among his followers—myself and Andrew, James and John included—to assist him in preaching and in casting out demons, so that a greater number could be reached. We were sent off in pairs to preach the same message of repentance; and we too were able to expel demons and work many cures.

"In an effort to counter his popularity, the scribes sought out Jesus' family and friends, and convinced some of them that he had gone mad, hoping that they would take charge of him and remove him from Galilee. On hearing of their arrival, he said 'Who are my mother and my brothers? Whoever does the will of God is brother and sister and mother to me.' Some scribes even came up from Jerusalem and accused him of being possessed himself, of casting out demons by the help of Satan rather than by God. That accusation *really* set him off! 'If Satan has suffered such mutiny in his ranks, his power is at an end; he cannot endure,' was Jesus' reply—to the delight of the crowds. And then he said, 'Every sin and all the blasphemies men utter will be forgiven them, but whoever blasphemes against the Holy Spirit will never be forgiven.' This outraged the scribes even more; they knew he was speaking of them, of their continuing denial of the source of his authority despite the miracles they had witnessed."

"But why should ascribing to Satan the works of God be unforgiveable?" I asked—wondering whether Paul, who by that definition might himself be deemed a blasphemer of the Holy Spirit prior to his conversion, would disagree.

"Do you recall, Mark, the traditional teaching regarding those who are to have no share in the world to come? Included on the list are 'those who say that the Torah is not from God.' Not those who merely believe this, but those who *say* it. And why? Perhaps it is more than the need for an utterance in order to produce the evidence to convict; perhaps also it is because of the capacity of such words to lead others astray. Jesus had the same concern. It was one thing for the scribes who were shown the truth to deny in their own hearts that God was acting through him. It was quite another for them to attempt to convince others. To Jesus, the matter was quite simple; you were either with him or against him depending on whether you accepted the divine source of his power and message, or spoke out against it. And he once said that anyone whose slander of the source of his power caused any believer to reject him would be better off plunged into the sea with a millstone around his neck!"

"How ironic that blasphemy against the Spirit, of all sins, should be declared unforgivable. Was not Jesus himself convicted and put to death, as the story has been told, on a charge of blasphemy—specifically, for claiming in front of the Sanhedrin to be the Son of God?"

"Blasphemy is reputed to be the charge; but whether he explicitly claimed to be the Son of God, I cannot testify. Certainly I did not hear it myself. The night he was arrested and taken before the Sanhedrin, I followed at a distance, all the way to the high priest's courtyard. But I was too far away to hear the testimony being adduced against him, or any response he may have uttered. All I could hear from the courtyard was the high priest and others crying 'Blasphemy!' and tearing their robes. So, perhaps he did say something which they interpreted as claiming to be the Son of God."

"You seem skeptical of this, Peter."

"I am. The penalty for blasphemy is stoning, not crucifixion, which is solely a Roman method of execution usually reserved for rebels and seditionists. Jesus was ultimately condemned, then, for a capital crime against Rome. A claim to divinity by a Jew is surely not such a crime, if indeed it would be viewed by the Romans as a crime at all rather than with simple bemusement."

Knowing Paul's insistence on the divinity of Jesus, I was anxious to press Peter further on his own view. "What, then, do you make of his forgiving the sins of the paralytic; was he not claiming an authority reserved exclusively for God, as the scribes believed?"

"Can God not delegate such power to a man? Surely He can! I am not prepared to make the same inference made by the scribes, Mark. Remember that John proclaimed his own baptism as being for the forgiveness of sins; yet no one suggested that John laid any claim to divinity in so doing."

"It is written in the parchments that Jesus once challenged a rich man who had called him 'good' by saying that no one is good but God alone. What are we to make of that question?"

"Well, does that not suggest his own view that he was *not* God?"

"It could as easily mean that he was testing the extent of the man's faith in him *as* God; don't you agree?"

"Come now, Mark! What possible basis could this rich Jew have had to reach such a conclusion in the first place—or Jesus, to ascribe it to him?"

"None, I agree; but perhaps he was using the man's question as a rhetorical device, to plant a seed in the minds of his listeners that would be developed later."

Although it was obvious to both of us that I was reading more into this passage than it could reasonably support, Peter was both patient and kind with me in his response. "I agree that there is much he said, and much written in the parchments, that must be left to interpretation. But we should be slow to construe ambiguous words spoken by a Jew as a claim to divinity. God's revelation to Israel that He is One cannot easily be reconciled with such a notion. Polytheists may declare that a man is truly a god, as the Romans have said of Julius Caesar and of Octavian Augustus, or as the Egyptians said of the ancient Pharaohs. Jews cannot easily make the same pronouncement, and I am not prepared to make it here."

"I take it, then, that *you* never heard him claim to be God's son?"

"Never once; not even in the adoptive sense of the word. Indeed, if he had made such a claim in the literal sense, we might have worshipped at his feet! 'Son of Man' was his favorite way of characterizing himself, a phrase that the prophet Ezekiel employed to emphasize the distinction *between* God and mortal man. Certainly the Pharisees and the scribes, who accused him of a great many things, never made any accusation that by calling himself 'Son of Man' Jesus was claiming to be divine. The phrase would for them have been a direct reference to his humanity and nothing more—as in the Psalm, *'What is man that you should be mindful of him, or the son of man that you should care for him.'* Of course, that is not to say that Jesus himself meant the phrase as a description of his humanity; after all, none of his listeners would have doubted that he was human, so why continually emphasize the point? But if he intended a different meaning, he never expressed it to us."

"Well, the Book of Daniel calls the one who is to come on the clouds of heaven and receive everlasting glory 'one like a Son of Man.' Perhaps, Peter, that was the association Jesus intended his listeners to draw. After all, the parchments quote him thus:

> *'For whoever is ashamed of me in this sinful generation, of him will the Son of Man also be ashamed, when he comes in the glory of his Father with the holy angels.'*

Does that not suggest a parallel between Jesus and Daniel's figure?" I inquired—suppressing the more natural reading of Jesus' quote as drawing a distinction between the first-person "me" and the third-person "Son of Man" as two different persons.

"Perhaps, Mark, but such an association would not get us very far; none of his listeners would have any reason to think that Daniel's

'Son of Man' was divine, either. Indeed, Daniel goes on to relate that the angel Gabriel used the appellation 'Son of Man' in referring to Daniel himself, so the phrase could hardly have carried a reference to divinity in Daniel's mind.

"I suspect it did not in Jesus' mind, either, for he once suggested the exact opposite meaning of 'Son of Man.' When the twelve of us plucked some grain to eat from a field we were passing through, Jesus responded to an accusation from some Pharisees that we were violating the prohibition against working on the Sabbath. He said to them, 'The Sabbath was made for mankind, not mankind for the Sabbath; so the Son of Man is lord even of the Sabbath.' Looking beyond the overtones of his claim of authority in interpreting the Law, it would be hard to interpret 'Son of Man' in that statement as anything but human, don't you think?"

"I suppose so," I responded, wondering why a group of Pharisees would be in a grain field on the Sabbath to begin with. "Then what did he mean by the phrase?"

"As I say, he never defined it. We who followed him eventually came to think of 'Son of Man' as shorthand for the Messiah, the descendant from the line of David foretold of old. Of course, my view of the Messiah at the time was that of the Psalms of Solomon—a human king, like David, who would restore the kingdom of Israel. To my knowledge, no scripture explicitly states that the Messiah will be divine."

"We do have Micah's prophesy that from Bethlehem shall come forth 'one who is to rule in Israel, whose origin is from old, from ancient days.' Could that be such a reference?"

Peter shook his head. "I know the rumor has circulated that Jesus was born in Bethlehem, but he never said that to me. As far as I knew, he was from Nazareth. In any event, you take the passage out of context; if Micah were referring to a divine being here, surely he would not have gone on to portray this ruler as acting in the name of 'the Lord *his* God.' At any rate, I claim no particular insight on this Scripture as applied to Jesus, regardless of his birthplace."

"Paul apparently does. He wrote in his letter to Timothy that Jesus existed before the world began. Do you suppose he could be right?"

Peter's lips pursed slightly. "That is certainly a remarkable notion—although perhaps not in Paul's mind. All I can attest is that I never heard Jesus claim eternal preexistence."

"What of the story about Jesus' preaching in the temple precincts in Jerusalem, asking the crowd how the scribes could claim that the Messiah is David's son when David himself writes 'The Lord said to my Lord: sit at my right hand until I make your enemies your footstool'? Did not Jesus ask, 'If David himself addressed him as Lord, how could he be David's son?' Could he have been hinting here at his own preexistence?

"I doubt it. For one thing, I do not accept the premise that a son cannot be lord over his father unless he somehow existed *before* his father. Thus David himself, on being anointed king, became lord even over his own father Jesse. But more importantly, I hesitate to conclude that Jesus' reference to David's son was meant as a reference to himself, for that would have been inconsistent with the command he gave us to keep his Messianic identity a secret."

"A secret?"

"Indeed. He once asked us who we thought he was. When I answered that he was the Messiah, he sternly ordered us not to tell anyone."

"If he believed himself to be the Messiah, divine or not, why would he want his identity kept secret?"

"Because such a claim would inevitably have been misinterpreted, Mark. A political Messiah, a king to restore the kingdom of Israel on earth, was what everyone would understand by the term, just as we who followed him did at first—and Jesus was no zealot seeking to overthrow Roman rule. Yet who could blame us for expecting him to bring about such an overthrow? Here was a man who could calm the wind and the seas with a single word; surely he could accomplish at least as much as the judges and kings of olden days who overcame superior military might through the power of God.

"But when we first acknowledged him to be the Messiah, he immediately began to tell us of the suffering and death he would endure. We resisted that notion. It took us some time to comprehend this and to refocus our expectations of what the Messiah would accomplish. His suffering and death are incomprehensible in political terms; they make sense only in terms of the redemptive work that permits entry into a heavenly kingdom."

Peter paused for a moment, and then looked straight at me. "I have devoted my life to furthering that redemptive work, by bringing the gospel to as many as I can. But I need your help to do more, Mark. When we reach Rome, you must help me to write down my memories of Jesus. I do not want them to die with me."

My excitement at the notion was immediate, and much more intense than when Timothy had suggested such a mission for me at the beginning of our voyage. "It would be my great honor, Peter! Your memories will *not* die with you. But do not talk of death. You have many years still ahead of you."

"Do I?" Peter made no further reply; he simply gazed at the hills in the distance, a look of both sadness and apprehension on his face. And the rest of the way to Silvium, amid the clicking of hooves and creaking of the wheels, no words were exchanged between us.

He knew.

Chapter 14

The next day's journey was to Venusia, the birthplace of the great Roman poet Horace. In one of his famous odes, Horace had written *"dum loquimur, fugerit invida aetas: carpe diem"*—"Even as we speak, this envious age is fleeing from us; seize the day." Yesterday's unspoken portent weighed heavily on my mind, and a sense of urgency in learning what I could from Peter about Jesus' ministry pressed me to press him.

"Will you tell me more, Peter, about the miracles Jesus performed?"

Peter had on his belt a *kophinos*, the small basket-like pouch that orthodox Jews filled with kosher food and carried on their travels, lest they find themselves in Gentile territory at meal time with only Gentile food available. He removed it, cupped it in his hands, and began to smile and nod. "Do you remember the story about the prophet Elisha multiplying twenty loaves given by one man to feed a hundred, with leftovers besides?"

"I do indeed."

"Once, on the shores of the Sea of Galilee, Jesus had been preaching to the crowd. It was late, the area was remote, and most of the crowd had no food. Jesus was concerned about sending them home hungry, so he told the twelve of us to give them some food. While each of us had his *kophinos*, most were already empty. And we were hungry, too. So we said to him, 'We have but only a few loaves of bread and a couple of fishes among us, and there must be five thousand people here! Where can we find enough food out here to give to so many?'

"Jesus told the crowd to sit down in groups, and had us place our food before him. Hungry though we were ourselves, we did as he asked. He took our food, gave thanks to God, broke the bread and divided it and the fish more or less equally into each of our twelve baskets, and told us to distribute it to the groups. Our dozen *kophinoi* were passed out to the crowd, handed from one person to the next. When all had eaten, we collected the left over fragments—and the twelve baskets came back to us completely full! We couldn't understand what had happened. It didn't make sense. I know my *kophinos* was almost empty when I handed it to Jesus, and full at the end."

"It is written in the parchments, '*The measure you give will be the measure you receive, and more will be given you besides.*' Perhaps this miracle was an affirmation of that statement."

"Indeed, Mark. I understood only later the connection between human charity as the raw material for fashioning miracles, and the benefit that those miracles returned to the giver. Perhaps Jesus could have created food out of nothing if he had wanted, but it pleased him to use our sacrifice to initiate this miracle."

"Did you observe the multiplication of loaves and fishes directly—I mean, did you actually see food materialize out of thin air?"

"No, Mark. And when I have told others about this miracle, some have said that the crowd must already have had a lot of bread and fish, so that there really was no actual multiplication. But I ask in response, which is the greater miracle: creating food out of nothing, or a spontaneous outpouring of charity by thousands, to share what they had with their neighbors? Either way, it was out of charity that abundance was returned. The Scriptures say that Elisha once commanded a poor widow to pour out her last jug of oil into many borrowed vessels, and then sell the oil to satisfy her husband's creditors—and afterward she and her children were able to live on what remained. So it is with us. If we give all that we have to the service of God, the remains of our gifts return to us, and are more than enough to sustain us afterwards."

"Was charity often a prelude to his miracles?"

"To many of them, yes; but to many others, the prelude was faith. The cure of the blind beggar Bartimaeus, for example, who recognized Jesus more clearly than those with two good eyes! We were leaving Jericho, heading toward Jerusalem, and he cried out 'Jesus, Son of David, have pity on me!' He refused to be silenced by the crowds, and persisted in shouting out 'Son of David,' until Jesus called him over and asked what he wished done for him. 'Rabonni, I want to see,' was his response. Jesus replied 'Go; your faith has healed you.' And Bartimaeus immediately regained his sight.

"Sometimes he healed those whose faith in him was so great as to embolden them to defy law and custom. Once, when he was out in the region of Tyre in upper Galilee, a Gentile woman found him and begged him to cure her daughter, who was possessed by an unclean spirit. He said 'Let the children be fed first, for it is not right to take the children's bread and throw it to the dogs.' She answered, 'Yes Lord, but even the dogs under the table eat the children's crumbs.' He replied, 'For saying this, you may go; the demon has left your daughter.'

"Another time, a woman afflicted by constant menstrual hemorrhaging pressed her way through the crowds to touch Jesus' clothing, ignoring her social stigma and ritual impurity, and risking grave punishment for defiling those she might touch. The instant she touched his clothing, she was healed. Jesus must have felt that his healing power had gone out from him, for he turned to see who in the crowd had done this. With great fear and trembling she fell at his feet and admitted what she had done. He simply replied, 'Daughter your faith has cured you; go in peace, free of this affliction.'

"The opposite was true as well; where faith was lacking, he seemed less able to work miracles. Once, in his own hometown, those who had known him since birth were scandalized at him, and did not believe. 'A prophet is not without honor except among his own kin,' he said—and he could perform no miracles there, except for laying his hands on a few who were ill and curing them."

"What do you suppose was his greatest healing miracle?"

Peter did not hesitate in giving his answer. "Do you remember the story of Elisha raising the son of a Shunammite woman from the dead?"

"I do. She went out to Elisha, fell at his feet, and insisted that he return home with her, even though her child was already dead. And Elisha did so, and raised the boy."

"Precisely. One time, the leader of one of the local synagogues came out to Jesus, fell at his feet and begged him to come with him and cure his daughter, who was gravely ill. 'Please come and lay your hands on her, that she may get well, and live,' he pleaded. Jesus immediately helped him to his feet and set off with him to his house. We all followed. Along the route we were met by some of his servants, who told the man 'Your daughter is already dead. Why trouble the Teacher further?'—for up to this point Jesus had only healed the sick, not raised the dead. But Jesus ignored the servants and said to the man, 'Have no fear; only have faith.' And he allowed only James, John and I to accompany them back to the man's house.

"When we arrived, people were already mourning, weeping and wailing loudly. Jesus said to them 'Why are you making such a din with all this wailing? The girl is not dead; she is asleep.' They ridiculed him, but he simply put them all outside, and along with us and the child's father and mother, went in where the girl was. He took her by the hand and said, 'Little girl, arise!' And immediately she stood up and walked. We were completely amazed! 'Get her something to eat,' he told the parents."

"But was she truly dead, or merely asleep?"

"There is no question in my mind that that she was dead. Before entering the room he had said 'she is asleep' only to keep the event from becoming known as a true resurrection—which would have brought even more notoriety upon himself. He told us at the time not to let anyone know what had happened.

"He often tried to keep his miracles from being widely reported, particularly early in his ministry. In the region of the Ten Cities, the crowds once brought a deaf-mute to Jesus and begged him to cure the man. He took the man off by himself away from the crowd, and healed him out of their sight, enjoining him not to tell anyone—as if the man could help himself! Another time, in Bethsaida, the crowds brought a blind man to Jesus and begged him to touch the man. Jesus took the man outside the village, where he restored the man's sight—and then told him 'Do not even go back into the village.' But of course, the man did go back."

"Why would he not want his miracles to be widely known? Was it for fear that the people might come to believe, as Bartimaeus had, that he was the Messiah?"

"I doubt it. In none of the messianic prophesies are healing miracles associated with the Messiah, so his being the Messiah cannot easily be inferred from such miracles. In truth, I cannot tell you why he favored secrecy as to his miracles. Perhaps it was out of humility; he was never one to court notoriety or personal glory. Perhaps he simply did not like crowds. And at times, his miracles were witnessed only by the twelve of us because no one else was nearby."

"But why limit the witnesses to the young girl's raising just to James, John and yourself, rather than all twelve of you? Why keep it from the other nine?"

"I cannot say. Perhaps the reason is tied up with another event a few months later, that only the three of us were privileged to witness."

"What happened?"

An air of reverence came over Peter as he told me the story. "It was during the Feast of Booths. Jesus asked the three of us to ascend a high mountain with him. There on the summit, he was transformed before our eyes, his face glowing with the brightness of the sun, and his clothes shone dazzling white! Suddenly two angelic figures appeared next to him, and began conversing with him; we thought they were Elijah and Moses! We were overcome with awe, but could not turn away. I started babbling like an idiot; I think I even offered to erect booths for the three of them! All at once a cloud overshadowed them, and we heard thunder like the voice of God from heaven. Then just as suddenly, the other two figures disappeared in the cloud and only Jesus stood there before us. James, John and I looked at each other with total bewilderment, silently seeking confirmation that all three of us had indeed just seen the same thing, that it was not imagined."

"But what did this transfiguration mean?"

"It was a foretaste of the glory that would be his after his resurrection, Mark. He had said that some of us would live to see the coming reign of God on earth, and now he was showing the three of us, in some small way, what that reign of power would look like. Jesus was revealing himself to us as able to invoke the power to overcome death, the power to summon the souls of the dead to return to their bodies, as with the young girl. And as we descended the mountain, he instructed us to tell no one what we had seen until he himself rose from the dead.

"But at the time, the two brothers and I did not understand what we had seen as a foreshadowing of his resurrection—how *could* we?—and while we discussed among ourselves what his own 'rising from the dead' might mean and pondered the notion that he must die first in order to rise, we kept the miraculous vision to ourselves as requested."

"Did you ever ask Jesus why he wanted the three of you to keep what you had seen from the other disciples?"

"No." Peter sighed, discerning a hint of skepticism on my face. "I am well aware that any reference to such commands of secrecy will be viewed by doubters as a convenient cover for the mere fabrication of these events by his followers. But I speak the truth. And in this case, it was obvious to anyone who was waiting below that *something* extraordinary had happened to Jesus on that mountain."

"What do you mean?"

"We arrived at the base of the mountain to find the others arguing with some scribes, in front of a gathering crowd. The scribes were deriding the disciples for being unable to cure a boy possessed by a deaf and mute spirit. But once the crowd spotted Jesus, they were awestruck, for his face was still radiant—just as the scriptures say of Moses' face when he descended Mount Sinai with the tablets of the covenant. 'He has been speaking with God,' some of them said among themselves.

"When the deaf-mute spirit caught sight of Jesus, it immediately threw the boy into convulsions. The boy's father explained that it had possessed the boy since early childhood, often hurling him into fire or into water, nearly killing him. The father pleaded with Jesus, 'Please help us if you can.' 'If I *can*, you say? Everything is possible for he who believes,' Jesus told him. 'I do believe!' the man responded. 'Help my *lack* of faith.'

"Then Jesus commanded the spirit to depart the boy, and it did so with a shout, leaving the boy as still as a corpse. Everyone thought he was dead. Then Jesus helped him to his feet and sent him and his father on their way, to the amazement of the crowd!"

"Why were the other disciples not able to expel the spirit?"

"We asked Jesus that same question later. He told us that this type can only be driven out by prayer. He was reminding us, I think, not to lose sight of whose power was being employed to perform such miracles. Lest we might think it was through power granted to *us* by God, Jesus was saying that it was by *God's* power, which we may pray *Him* to exercise. Otherwise," Peter said simply, but with a hint of a smile, "pride gets in the way."

Prayer, it occurred to me, was precisely what I myself needed more of, and pride less of. Never once had I been the vehicle for performing any miracle, and perhaps this was the reason. Or, perhaps my faith simply was not strong enough. More than likely it was a bit of both. I recalled the relationship between prayer and faith set out in one of Jesus' sayings recorded in the Parchments:

'I give you my word, if you are ready to believe that you will receive whatever you ask for in prayer, it shall be done for you.'

And as our cart rambled toward Venusia, I felt an affinity with the father of the deaf-mute boy. Silently, I prayed: "I *do* believe! Help my lack of faith!"

Chapter 15

The next morning we proceeded on to Beneventum, the half way point between Tarentum and Rome. I hoped my discussions with Peter, however, were not nearly half finished. As thrilled as I was by the prospect of writing down for posterity Peter's accounts of our Lord's ministry, clearly there was much that I personally could learn from Peter's reminiscences. Part of me wanted our journey to be extended, despite the discomfort of the trip.

This day was to be more uncomfortable than most. The early morning sun was already unusually hot, and by afternoon it would be brutal. We had not seen a drop of rain since reaching Italy, and again today there was not a cloud in sight on this shadeless stretch of the Appian Way.

Although Peter was surely suffering from the heat as much as I, his voice and his countenance, if not his brow, showed no signs of it. The day was spent recounting Jesus' parables rather than his miracles, and I was fascinated to hear them and ponder their meaning.

"One time," Peter began, "Jesus was teaching beside the sea, and the crowd gathering about him grew so great that he was obliged to get into a boat and cast out a short distance, preaching to the whole crowd on the land. And he taught them thus about the kingdom of God: 'A farmer went out to sow, and as he sowed, some seed fell along the footpath, where the birds came and devoured it. Other seed fell on rocky ground, where it had little soil, and immediately it sprouted, having no depth of soil; but when the sun rose it was scorched, and since it had no root it withered away. Other seed fell among thorns which grew up and choked it, and it yielded no grain. Finally other seeds fell onto good soil and brought forth grain, growing up and increasing and yielding thirtyfold and sixtyfold and a hundredfold.'

"Afterwards, apart from the crowd, we asked him about the parable. He said 'Do you not understand it? How then will you understand others like it? To you has been given the secret of the kingdom of God, but for those outside everything is in parables; so that they may indeed see but not perceive, and may indeed hear but not understand, lest they should repent and be forgiven.'"

At once I recognized Jesus' echoing of the prophet Isaiah: *"You are to make the heart of this people sluggish, to dull their ears and close their eyes; else their eyes will see, their ears hear, their heart understand, and they will turn and be healed."* I had always had great difficulty with the passage. Directing Isaiah to preach to a people who would not understand his message seemed pointless—as pointless as casting seed onto soil which cannot sustain it. More than that, the passage had the flavor of determinism to it, which I had always found distasteful.

"But why would Jesus not want everyone to understand, Peter? Why would he not welcome universal repentance and forgiveness? And if he intended to preclude outsiders from comprehending it, why not simply withhold the parable from the crowd, and save it for his inner circle?"

"Perhaps the real answer lies within the parable itself. The explanation Jesus gave of it was this: 'The sower sows the word of God. Those along the pathway where the word is sown hear it, but Satan immediately comes and takes away the word which is sown in them. Those upon rocky ground, when they hear the word, immediately receive it with joy, but with no root in themselves they endure for only a while; then, when tribulation or persecution arises on account of the word, immediately they fall away. Those among thorns hear the word, but when the cares of the world, and the delight in riches, and the desire for other things, enter in and choke the word, it proves unfruitful. But those that were sown upon the good soil are the ones who hear the word and accept it and bear fruit, thirtyfold and sixtyfold and a hundredfold.'"

"So, why not just say *that*, rather than obscuring the message in a parable and confounding much of his audience?"

"Because only by use of the parable could he encourage the faithful while not alienating the faithless. To be accepted, the word of God must first be truly understood, not superficially through the literal meaning of the words—as by those who 'see but do not perceive, hear but do not understand'—but on a level which internalizes the message and grasps its call for repentance and forgiveness. That level of understanding comes with faith, the same faith which gives sight to the blind and hearing to the deaf, as in the miracles we spoke of yesterday. Those whose faith is sufficient to accept the truth lying within the parable are the only ones meant to receive that truth anyway, so veiling the message in a parable which only they can decipher does no harm; nor does veiling it from nonbelievers, for it would not take root with them anyway. If it is to bear fruit, the word of God must be accepted with faith, for in no other way can it result in resistance to Satan, to trials, and to the temptations of the world."

"But if Jesus deliberately obscured his teaching so that only the faithful would understand it, why did his disciples not understand the parable initially?"

"Because he was teaching us his teaching *method* first, so that we could then gradually absorb the message within. This was his way of speaking publicly, yet selectively revealing the secret of the kingdom of God to only those whom he chose."

"And what is that secret, Peter?"

"That God's reign is already here, growing in the hearts of believers. The Zealots, who seek immediate rebellion against Rome to restore the kingdom of Israel, misunderstand the nature of that reign. God's kingdom is indeed one of great power, but it is the power of love rather than of military might. Many are blinded to this simple truth, because they count only physical prosperity, political control and military power as the attributes of an earthly kingdom. They set their hearts on such mundane desires even though they view themselves as religious, and they fail to appreciate the possibility that even on earth God can install a kingdom whose hallmark is love. To them, an earthly kingdom entails a king, a successor to David, who reigns with God-given authority over peoples and lands and whose armies protect the nation from its enemies.

"If history teaches anything, it is that earthly kingdoms do not remain at peace for long. Both the rulers and the ruled soon become discontented. In the rulers, pride leads to the desire for further dominance, further accumulation of wealth and power, and with such greed there comes no rest; the pleasure of riches and honor leads to insatiable vanity. In the ruled, the desire for autonomy fosters jealousies and anger, for they live in obedience out of necessity rather than choice. They become discontented, and are quickly tempted to take what advantage they can of others, or of carnal desires and sensual pleasures—and their unhappiness returns when they find that following their passions has not led to peace. But the citizens of the kingdom of love, although poor and humble, live in a *world* of peace. If they have material things or temporal power, they do not glory in them, but in God who is all-powerful. They do not boast of personal stature or of physical beauty, knowing that such qualities do not last. When they act with charity it is genuine, not motivated by self-interest or hope of reward or recognition. They find true contentment in the love of God and neighbor.

"This is the secret Jesus has revealed: that God's kingdom of love is here, now. The word of God he sows *is* the word of love, and it is truly powerful. In the fertile soil of an honest and loving heart, the word of God germinates and matures—'like a mustard seed,' was Jesus' analogy. 'When sown upon the ground it is the smallest of all seeds; yet once sown it grows into the greatest of all shrubs,' he said. Have we not seen such immense growth ourselves, Mark, in the spreading of this message of love throughout the nations?"

"We have indeed!"

"He also likened the kingdom of God to one who scatters seed on the ground, goes to sleep, and rises the next day to find that the seed has sprouted—he knows not how. 'The earth produces of itself, first the stalk, then the head, then the full grain in the head. But when the grain is ripe,' he said, 'immediately he goes with his sickle to reap the harvest.' And when the time is ripe at the end of days, so too will the faithful be gathered into God's presence."

"Did Jesus say when those end times would come?"

Peter shook his head. "Andrew and I, and Zebedee's sons, once asked him that very question. I remember the setting very well: the four of us, the first four to be called, were sitting with him on the Mount of Olives, gazing across the valley at the Temple in the distance. He told us he did not know when the end would come; no one did, not even the angels in heaven, only God. He taught us: 'Beware, and keep alert, for you do not know when the time will come. It is like a man who leaves home to go on a journey and puts his servants in charge, each with an assigned task—and charges his gatekeeper to be on the watch. Be vigilant, for you do not know when the master of the house will return, whether in the evening, or at midnight, or at cockcrow or dawn; lest he find you asleep when he comes suddenly.'

"When we asked him what signs would precede the end times, he told us to expect strange celestial events—the sun and moon darkened, stars falling from the sky, and finally, 'the Son of Man coming in clouds with great power and glory, sending out the angels to gather his elect from the ends of the earth to the ends of heaven.'

"He predicted many other things that would happen before these end days—wars, earthquakes, famines and other tribulations. He pointed across the valley to the Temple, and said of it 'Not one stone will be left standing upon another; all will be thrown down.' Then he told us, 'But when you see the desolating sacrilege standing where it ought not to be, then those in Judea must flee to the mountains at once; whoever is on a housetop must not go down into the house to retrieve anything; whoever is in a field must not go back to get a coat. Woe to women who are pregnant or are nursing infants in those days. Pray that it may not be in winter. For there will be suffering such as has never been witnessed since the beginning of creation, nor will be again!' Just as the angels warned Lot, on the eve of destruction of Sodom and Gomorrah, to flee for his life up into the hills without stopping or looking back, Jesus warned us to do the same."

"What do you suppose he meant by 'desolating sacrilege?'" I asked, recalling the book of Daniel's use of the same phrase to refer to what the Seleucid king Antiochus Epiphanes had done several centuries ago—setting up an altar to Zeus in the Temple and sacrificing swine on it, touching off the Maccabean revolt.

"He was not specific, so I cannot be sure, but I suspect we will know it when we see it. I once thought his words were a prediction of something that happened when you were still a young man in Jerusalem, Mark. Perhaps you recall it. The Emperor Gaius, who fancied himself a god and had nothing but bitterness for the Jews who refused to acknowledge him as such, sought to have a statute of himself fashioned and erected in the Temple within the Holy of Holies—something which would have led to steadfast resistance and untold devastation and misery for the Jews, had the Emperor not been persuaded by the supplications and entreaties of Agrippa and others to change his mind and avoid bloodshed.

"That was twenty four years ago, and mercifully, the profanity of such a statue 'where it ought not to be' did not occur. But perhaps the phrase was just a metaphor for the idolatry of evil ultimately consuming the Temple. Nero is no less egomaniacal than was Gaius; such an affront to the sanctity of God's people could yet occur. The strain of relations between Rome and Jerusalem has waxed and waned, but I am quite sure that eventually it will flare again to the point of outright war. Indeed, the Zealots are virtually crying out for such hostilities even now. I have no doubt that when this comes to pass, it will have disastrous results for Israel. When Jerusalem falls to Babylon a second time, those of us who have been warned will know that the end days are upon us."

"When I write down your memories of what the Lord has said and done, Peter, should I not warn everyone of this?"

"Yes, but take care to preserve his cipher 'desolating sacrilege.' Those for whom the warning is meant will recognize it when it occurs; from the rest, it will remain hidden. That was ever his way, his reason for using parables, and you would do well to adopt it here lest you help incite in the enemies of Israel the very actions being veiled by the metaphor!"

"Your point is well taken, Peter. But do you really think these things will all happen during Nero's reign?"

"It would not surprise me in the least, Mark. Jesus told us, 'Learn a lesson from the fig tree: when its branches become tender and it puts forth leaves, you know that summer is near. So also, when you see these things I have described taking place, you will know that the end is near, at the very gates where you have been charged to remain watchful. I tell you truly, this generation will not pass away until all these things have taken place.' Surely 'this generation' is close to passing away now."

Peter's words harkened back to the saying recorded in the parchments that Timothy and I had discussed at the outset of our journey: *'I tell you truly, there are some standing here who will not taste death until they see that the kingdom of God has come with power.'* At once I found myself questioning the logic of preserving Peter's memories for generations of future readers.

"Suppose you are right, and the end times are close. Does it make sense, then, for me to write at all?"

"Certainly it does! Surely God, no less than the Emperor Gaius, can be persuaded to forestall actions that lead to destruction, whether through the supplication of the faithful or otherwise. From Noah to Abraham to Moses and beyond, Scripture relates many examples of God relaxing His anger, deferring His vengeance and showing mercy for the sake of believers who entreat Him to stay His wrath. We cannot know whether that will happen again. If it were otherwise—if praying to God to alter His plan for the end times were a waste of breath—would Jesus have suggested praying that the end not come in winter?"

"I see your point."

"Then write you must, Mark. There could well be many future generations to write for."

With mixed emotions, I wondered whether that would be so.

Chapter 16

At dawn the next day we left Beneventum and headed west along the Appian Way toward Capua and ultimately Sinuessa, a resort on the seacoast known for its salubrious hot springs—although they had brought no health to the Emperor Claudius, who was murdered there ten years earlier. Claudius had married his scheming niece Agrippina, the grand-daughter of Augustus, and according to rumor she had Claudius poisoned in a plot to ensure that her son Nero would ascend the throne instead of Brittanicus, Claudius' son from his prior marriage. Her own ambition to rule from behind the scenes eventually became too much for Nero, who had her killed as well.

As our cart rambled out along the road, Peter picked up the story of Jesus' ministry with a discussion of the folly of ambition for position and glory.

"Let me tell you, Mark, of the time Jesus overheard the twelve of us debating which of us was the most important. He had just been telling us of his own impending humiliation and vindication—that the Son of Man was soon to be delivered into the hands of men, who would kill him, only to have him rise again. As incomprehensible as his statement was to us, we didn't ask him what he meant; instead, we argued amongst ourselves over which of us was worthy of leading the group after he was gone. Here was a man about to sacrifice his life, and all *we* could talk about was glorifying our own lives!

"When he asked us what we were arguing about, we were too ashamed to speak. But he knew. He sat us down, and calmly told us that whoever aspired to be first among us must make himself last, and the servant of all. 'Many who are first shall come last, and the last shall come first,' he said.

"I pointed out to him that we had put aside everything we held dear, family and property, in order to follow him. He assured us that all who did so would receive them back a hundredfold in the present age, and be rewarded with everlasting life in the age to come. But he also cautioned us not to adopt the attitude of one who sacrifices *because* of the hope of future reward. Selflessness, humility, even suffering; these are what make one great in God's eyes, which is reward enough.

"It is such a hard thing to grasp, Mark, this new way of thinking about greatness in terms of service and humility. And we did not grasp it at first; in our prideful need for recognition and status, Jesus' measure of greatness just fostered an argument over who among us had sacrificed the most and therefore was greatest as among ourselves.

"James and John—sons of thunder that they were!—had the audacity to request that they be allowed to sit next to Jesus, one at his left and the other at his right, when he came into his glory. So great was their ambition, they wanted to be like the two angelic figures that they had seen flanking Jesus on the mountain! He challenged them, 'Do you know what you are asking? Can you drink from the same cup that I am to drink, or be baptized in the same baptism of pain as I?' They were so bold as to reply that they could indeed do so. And fools that *we* were, the rest of us were indignant at their presumptuous play for superior rank! Again, he gently reminded us that a position of preeminence required service to the needs of all. He told us, 'Be not like the scribes, who parade around in their robes and seek out public respect, taking front seats in the synagogues and places of honor at banquets. It must not be like that with you.'"

"I take it, then, he did not grant the brothers' request?" I asked.

"He said he had no authority to do so; it was for God alone to reserve such places of honor for those He chose. But he did tell James and John that they would indeed drink from the same cup and be immersed in the same baptism as he." Peter's voice had a hint of apprehension in it. We both knew of James' fate—beheading, at the behest of Herod. What would happen to his brother John? Or, for that matter, to the rest of the twelve who were still alive?

"Did this answer stop the debate among you?" I inquired.

"As far as who among us was greatest, yes; but arrogance is a difficult thing to tame. Rather than lose our pride and self-importance, we simply shifted its focus toward our own group of twelve as being superior to others."

"How so?"

"Do you remember the story of Eldad and Medad, who prophesied in the camp of the Israelites when Moses and the seventy elders were gathered at the tent outside the camp—how Joshua complained to Moses that they should be stopped, and Moses rebuked him? In like manner, John complained to Jesus of someone not of our party, who was casting out demons in his name. 'We tried to stop him, Teacher,' he said. But Jesus said, 'Do not stop him; for no one can do such things in my name and at the same time speak ill of me. Whoever is not against us is for us.'

"I myself have learned this lesson all too slowly," Peter continued solemnly. "In fact, there was a time when I was jealous of Paul, of the great following he had developed among the Gentiles."

I was completely taken aback by this admission; Peter, a rock of the faith, the acknowledged leader of the original disciples of the Lord, jealous of another's success in winning souls! It seemed so incongruous to my image of the man. "You have no cause for jealousy, Peter," I protested. "You are as great an apostle as any; I have seen with my own eyes that you are! Why, look at what you accomplished back in Tarentum just a few days ago—and many other times before then."

"Yet I am the *least* of the Lord's apostles, Mark."

"You are wrong, Peter! Indeed, Paul claimed that title for himself when he wrote to the Corinthian church, because he once persecuted the followers of the Lord."

"Ah, yes, I have read his letter. Paul's self-effacement makes a pretense of humility, belied by his urging the Corinthians to be imitators of himself. In any event, what he did before his conversion, he did in ignorance of the truth. But I, I who learned at the Lord's feet and purported to serve and follow him, have committed a greater sin than persecution. In his final hours, I deserted him."

"What are you *talk*ing about?"

Peter's eyes saddened. "We shall speak of this another time, Mark. For now, it is enough simply to say that we must be ever vigilant against pride and jealousy, for humility does not come naturally to us. The proof of this is that upon discovering humility to be a virtue greatly prized in the kingdom of heaven, we often seek the prize by declaring ourselves the most humble! That is itself a prideful declaration."

"I appreciate the conundrum; but humility can be pressed too far, Peter. Audacity in service of the Lord, for example, I would count as a good thing. Paul has often said that one must be bold in preaching the Way and in decrying false teachings, even at the risk of appearing audacious, for boasting in the service of God gives offense only to the ungodly."

"And Paul is the master of such boasting, Mark. He is fond of listing all of the sufferings, the imprisonments and beatings he has endured in that service. Such arrogance comes from having convinced himself that his teachings are beyond reproach, are presentations of absolute truth. He tolerates no disagreement on any issue of faith regardless of whether there is fair ground for disagreement, and regardless of whether there was any instruction on the matter by Jesus himself, in whose actual words Paul seems to take little interest, despite his recent request for the parchments. For my part, I find that I cannot be so presumptuous. There is much which remains uncertain, and while we remain on this earth the limitations of our knowledge ought to be admitted candidly, with a spirit of humility. It is that spirit which Jesus bade us to adopt, and as my years advance, I am finally beginning to heed that request."

"But do you and Paul really disagree on very much?"

"Oh, I suppose we do on a number of things, some significant, some less so. But as to much of what he teaches, I am simply unsure. Paul seems to have worked out an extended theology of the cross and its implications, and while he may well be right as to most, even all, of his inferences, I am not prepared to say so. I just do not know. Is that disagreement? Call it such if you like. My concern is to be cautious in claiming too much as true, in clothing speculation as dogma without a sufficient grounding either in the teachings of Jesus or the workings of the Spirit. Paul exhibits no such concern."

"But how can you be sure that the Spirit is not working in Paul as well, when he preaches the gospel?"

"I can't. As I said, I simply do not know. But this much is certain; Paul's very boldness, his *lack* of humility, gives his message an advantage over any competing version whose proponents are restrained by *their* humility. As time goes on—if Jesus has not returned—it is *Paul's* theology which will ultimately become orthodoxy, *Paul's* teachings which will form and shape the beliefs of the church; not mine."

"No, Peter. Let me be the instrument for recording and spreading *your* message, as *you* know it. I promise you, I will be true to it no matter what Paul or others may teach!"

Peter looked at me silently for a moment, as a parent looks sympathetically and patiently at a child who is without understanding. Then he said tenderly, "I think I *will* tell you now about my denial of Jesus."

I sensed the importance of what was about to be revealed to me, and my pulse quickened. With a deep breath, Peter began:

"You know the story of Jesus' betrayal, how at supper on the night before he was to be crucified, he told the twelve of us that one of our group who had been plotting against him would betray him and hand him over to the chief priests—a prediction fulfilled that very night by Judas. But what you do not know is that he made a second prediction that night, of a second betrayal.

"After supper, we walked out toward the Mount of Olives. Along the way, he turned to us and said that after he was handed over, the rest of us would scatter with our faith shaken. I was indignant at this, and immediately protested that no matter who else might be shaken in their faith, it would not be so with me. And Jesus replied, "I assure you, Simon, this very night, before the cock crows twice, you will deny me three times.' 'Never!' I replied. 'Even if it means I must die with you, I will not deny you!' We all said so.

"Then we came to the olive grove at the foot of the hillside at Gethsemani, not far from your mother's house, where we had often retired to pray. He told us to sit and wait while he prayed, but then he asked James, John and me to go with him into the grove. We could see what distress he was in; he knew his time was at hand, waiting for his betrayer to arrive. And he asked us to remain with him and stay awake. He went a little further and kneeled to pray. But the hour was late, and I and the brothers could not keep our eyes open. The next thing I knew, Jesus was standing over me, saying 'Asleep, Simon? Could you not stay awake even for an hour? Be vigilant, and pray that you are not put to the test. The spirit is willing, but the flesh is weak.' Again he went to pray, and again we dozed off! He awakened us again, and in our embarrassment and exhaustion we did not know what to say to him. A *third* time he went off to pray, and a third time we fell asleep! 'Still sleeping?' he said this time. 'Rouse yourselves; the hour of my betrayal is here, and the Son of Man must now be handed over to the clutches of evil men.'"

"And did the cock then crow?" I asked, thinking that these must have been the three denials Peter was speaking of.

"I wish with all my heart that it had! If failing to stay awake had been my only failure that evening, I might be at peace with it. I should have done as he bade; I should have prayed that I would not be put to the test. But God saw fit to humble me again.

"As we were leaving the garden and joining up with the rest of the disciples, an armed crowd sent by the chief priests arrived, with Judas in the forefront. Jesus did not resist or attempt to flee; he let Judas come up to him and kiss him—a signal to the mob, I suppose— and then they seized him. Jesus said to them, 'You come to arrest me armed with swords and clubs as though I were a brigand; yet while I was within your reach daily, teaching in the temple precincts, you never saw fit to arrest me?' Someone—not one of us, for we were unarmed—drew a sword and brandished it, and in the confusion accidently hit the high priest's slave, cutting his ear. On seeing this we panicked, and we all scattered, all of us who that very evening had pledged to die with him! We deserted him just as he had predicted.

"After they took him, I followed at a safe distance to see what would happen. They brought him to the high priest's house, into one of the upper rooms. I was in the courtyard below, warming myself by the fire with the temple guards and trying to look inconspicuous even as I strained to hear. One of the high priest's servant girls observed me, and said to me 'You were with Jesus of Nazareth, too.'

'I don't know what you are talking about; what do you mean?' I responded, and quickly headed for the gateway. But she started to tell everyone in the courtyard, 'This man is one of them.' Again, I denied it. Then some of the bystanders picked up the theme, and accused me, saying 'You are certainly on of them; you're a Galilean, aren't you?' I swore to them, 'I do not even know the man you are talking about!' And at that moment," Peter said as his voice cracked and his eyes welled with tears, "I heard the cock crow."

I was stunned into silence by this confession. No word of encouragement could I mouth to offer any comfort here; that much was obvious. I waited for Peter to make some comment, *any* comment, on forgiveness, resolve, atonement—but he simply let the matter lie where it was. Suddenly my brash assurance that I would remain faithful to Peter's testimony no matter what may happen seemed petty and insignificant.

And in the somberness of the moment, I could not bring myself to tell Peter that I understood only too well—indeed, firsthand—the panic that he and the others felt at Jesus' arrest. I could not relate to him the truth that I had kept to myself and tried to repress since the age of twelve: that *I too had witnessed Jesus' arrest, that very night*!

The memories all came flooding back to me. I had been awakened from my sleep by the commotion in the garden below my bedroom window. Peering out, I saw a procession of several dozen torches heading back toward the city. I immediately went down to investigate without taking the time to dress, wrapping my linen sheet around me against the chilly night air. I quickly managed to outflank them, and from behind a tree I saw the man who was being led away with his hands tied behind him. In the glare of the full Passover moon and the flickering torchlight, I could discern no trace of emotion on his face—only those piercing eyes that somehow spotted me despite my perch in the shadows, and for a brief moment held me transfixed. Suddenly someone grabbed me from behind and began to shout to the others. Terrified, I broke free and ran off naked into the night, pursued only by the haunting image of what I had seen.

In one way or another, I have been running from that image ever since.

Chapter 17

After spending the night in Sinuessa, we set out for Tarracina further up the coast, and a day's journey from Rome. The dry heat of summer was beginning to take its toll on us, and on our horse as well. Even the trees and shrubs that lined the way were looking parched and withered. How welcome a bit of rain would be!

Peter must have been thinking the same thing. "Do you see those shriveled fig trees, Mark?" he asked. "There is a fig tree on the road from Bethany to Jerusalem which looks that way all the time, and bears no fruit. Not long before Jesus' death, we were traveling that road toward the City, when he spotted the tree from a distance and went over to it to see if it had any fruit. I guess he was hungry. Anyway, although the tree was quite healthy and in full foliage, it was not yet the season for figs, so he found none. Then he said to the tree, "Let no one ever eat your fruit again!' And the very next day, when we passed the same tree again, it was withered away almost to its roots. 'Look, Rabbi,' we said, 'the tree you cursed yesterday has withered!'"

"Why would he do such a thing?" I wondered aloud. That Jesus would forbid a tree from bearing fruit in the future just because, quite naturally, it had no fruit at the moment seemed unreasonable and out of character.

"He didn't explain why. But the episode recalls for me the parable he told of the seed that had no depth of soil, which quickly sprouted but then withered for lack of roots. I believe he saw in the fig tree a symbol of the Temple, whose ornate adornments are akin to a tree in full bloom, but from which there is no harvest because of the perversion of its purpose by those who exploit it for gain, divorcing it from its roots. For on the same day that he cursed the fig tree, such perversion of purpose elicited his condemnation of the Temple as well."

"Condemnation of the Temple?"

"Of what it had become through the perversions of those having charge of it, yes. Do you recall the very last words of the prophet Zechariah, in reference to the tribulations of Jerusalem? *'On that day there shall no longer be any merchant in the house of the Lord of hosts.'* When we arrived in the City, we entered the Temple precincts, and in the Court of the Gentiles he observed the merchants who sold sheep and doves for sacrifice, changing the pilgrims' profane coins into the required Tyrian silver coins, at a profit—all under the oversight of the Sanhedrin. He became incensed, angrier than I had ever seen him. He overturned the money-changers' tables and the stalls of those selling doves, and cried out 'This is a house of prayer for all peoples, and you have turned it into a den of thieves!'

"Then he told this parable to the sizeable crowd that had gathered: 'A man planted a vineyard, put a wall around it, dug a pit for the winepress and built a tower. Then he leased the vineyard to tenant farmers and went away on a journey. At harvest time he sent a servant to collect from them his share of the fruit of the vineyard. But they seized him, beat him and sent him away empty-handed. Then he sent another servant to them; they struck him on the head and treated him shamefully. He sent still another, and that one they killed. He sent many others; some of them they beat, others they killed. Lastly, he even sent his own beloved son, thinking that they would surely respect him. But the tenants said to one another "Here is the one who will inherit everything; come, let us kill him, and the inheritance will be ours!" Then they seized and killed the son as well, and dragged him outside the vineyard. What do you suppose the owner of the vineyard will do when his patience is at an end? He will come and destroy the tenants and turn the vineyard over to others.'

"You can imagine the stir all of this caused with the Sanhedrin. The scribes were outraged; everyone knew the parable referred to them, the stewards of the Temple who had rejected the prophets sent by God and would now merit His retribution. They would have arrested us on the spot, but for fear of the crowd they left us and went off.

"When we returned to the Temple the following day, we were accosted by the chief priests and scribes, and I thought we would certainly be taken into custody then. But when they asked Jesus on what authority he was doing these things—hoping to catch him in blasphemy—his clever response silenced them. 'Let me ask *you* a question,' he said, 'and if you answer it, I will tell you on what authority I do what I do. Tell me: was John's baptism of divine origin, or merely from men?' But they were afraid to answer. If they said 'divine,' Jesus would ask them, 'Then why did you not believe in it?' On the other hand, if they said 'merely human,' they would risk alienating the people, who viewed John as a prophet. So they said 'We do not know.' And Jesus replied, 'Then neither will I tell you on what authority I act.'

"Then they sent some Pharisees and Herodians, to try to trap him as he had trapped them. The two groups baited him, saying 'Teacher, we know you are a truthful man who is not concerned with worldly opinions, but teach God's way sincerely. Please mediate a dispute for us. Is it lawful to pay the emperor's poll tax? Are we to pay or not?' Jesus immediately saw the dilemma: if he answered that the tax should be paid, he would be seen as idolatrous by the Pharisees who opposed tribute to one who viewed himself as a god; and if he answered that it should not be paid, the Herodians would report him to the Roman authorities as inciting rebellion. Seeing their hypocrisy, he responded as cleverly as before: 'Why do you seek to test me? Bring me a coin, and let me see it!' When they gave him a silver denarius, he asked 'Whose image is this, and whose inscription?' 'Caesar's,' they replied. 'Then give to Caesar what is Caesar's, but give to God what is God's,' he said. Everyone was amazed at this answer.

"Next, some Sadducees attempted to trip him up on the Scriptures, and asked him 'Teacher, Moses has written: *If anyone's brother dies leaving a wife but no child, his brother must take the wife and produce a child for his brother.* There were seven brothers; and the eldest took a wife and then died, leaving no children. The second took her, but he too died childless. The same thing happened to the third—in fact, to all seven. Last of all, the woman died. At the resurrection when they all come back to life, whose wife will she be, seeing as all seven married her?' Jesus replied: 'You are badly mistaken, and fail to understand either the Scriptures or the power of God. Moses wrote thus so that a man might live on in his descendants; but after the resurrection that is unnecessary—a man lives on in himself, by the power of God. When people rise from the dead they neither marry nor are given in marriage, but live like angels in heaven.' Once again, they were silenced."

As Peter spoke, I thought back to my discussion with Timothy of the nature of the resurrected body being akin to that of an angel—and also to my presumption that the antediluvian "sons of God" mentioned in Genesis as having married human women were in fact angels. That latter hypothesis might need revision, I thought.

"When it became clear that they were unable to outsmart him," Peter continued, "the Sanhedrin plotted to do away with him, but because of his popularity they dared not act against him in public. Jerusalem was crowded for the Passover, which was only a couple of days away. They would wait until he was apart from the crowds. I am convinced that he knew this was about to happen, knew that his days were numbered."

"Why do you say so?"

"The following evening, while we were in Bethany dining at the house of Simon the Leper, a woman entered the dining room with an alabaster jar full of perfume made from expensive nard, worth maybe three hundred silver pieces. She broke the jar and began pouring its entire contents on Jesus' head. We were outraged at such an extravagant waste, and protested that it could have been sold and the money given to the poor. But Jesus said, 'Let her alone, and don't criticize her. The poor will always be in your midst, and you can be generous to them whenever you wish; but you will not always have me. She does me a kindness. By perfuming my body, she is preparing it for burial.' And with that, we all grew silent.

"The next day was the first day of the festival, and we asked him where he wanted us to prepare the Passover supper. 'Two of you go into the city,' he said. 'When you come upon a man carrying a water jar, follow him, enter whatever house he enters, and ask the owner "Where is the guest room where the Teacher may eat the Passover with his disciples?" He will take you up to a room already furnished for the meal. There, you will ready the meal for us.' And so it happened, precisely as he had said. That evening while we reclined at table for the Seder, he took a loaf of bread, gave thanks and broke it, and gave it to us. 'Take this,' he said, 'This is my body.' Later he took a cup of wine, gave thanks and passed it to us, saying 'This is my blood, the blood of the covenant, which is to be poured out on behalf of many. I solemnly assure you, I will never again drink of the fruit of the vine until the day I drink it new in the kingdom of God.' And indeed," Peter continued with a sigh, "he was right; that very night they came for him and took him away."

Trying to place myself in the room with them, I imagined the great sadness that must have been felt by the twelve on hearing this. "How did you bear hearing him declare that his death was at hand?" I asked.

"In truth, Mark, it was a somber moment; but the full import of his words did not register with me right away. I think we were all in denial to some extent."

"The bread and wine at that last supper, Peter; did anyone question what he meant by calling it his body and blood, or point out the Torah's prohibition against consuming blood?"

"In the solemnity of the moment, no one dared ask anything. We were expecting him to interpret the significance of each element of the Passover meal according to the annual ritual so familiar to us—unleavened bread signifying the flight of Israel, bitter herbs recalling its slavery, and so forth—but instead, he added a new tradition, interpreting the bread and wine in terms of his own death. He was about to leave us, and I see now that this was his means of communing with us in a way we could reenact and memorialize after he was gone, just as a Seder memorializes Israel's deliverance from Egypt. Before the next sunset he would be as broken as that loaf of bread, his blood poured out as the cup of wine—and through our consumption of the bread and wine, he was including us in his death, inviting us to share in it in a symbolic way."

"Was he not referring to the new covenant established by his blood as replacing the sacrifice offered in the Temple?"

"Ah, that is Paul talking!" Peter replied with a slight smile. "As I learned during my time in Corinth, Paul teaches that Jesus' blood replaces 'the blood of the covenant' that Moses took from the sacrificial offerings at Sinai and splashed on the Israelites to seal their promise to be faithful to the Law. All I can say is that I never heard Jesus describe his actions as instituting a *new* covenant. That is Paul's interpretation. It may well be the right one; it certainly fits quite well with his teaching that the Law has been supplanted. But Jesus himself never said anything quite so sweeping."

"Do you think he was declaring himself to be a new Passover sacrifice?"

"Not that I can see. If he intended to draw an analogy between his blood and the blood of the Passover lamb that the Israelites applied to their lintels and doorposts in Egypt, it was not expressed. Certainly he never suggested that the Passover lamb was a sacrifice for the expiation of sin. Nor is it part of our tradition to consider the Passover sacrifice as one of atonement."

"But what would be the point of sharing in his death by partaking of the bread and wine, if not for the forgiveness of sin? Surely it is by acknowledging communion with his sacrifice that we obtain that forgiveness!"

"I do not disagree with your conclusion, Mark; I am simply saying that if atonement is to be the significance of this ritual sharing of bread and wine, then *Yom HaKippurim* rather than Passover would be the sacrifice to analogize to. As befits a poor fisherman, I leave the commentary to others."

Once again Peter's humility reminded me of my own shortcomings, and I grew silent. In the distance I could see the town of Tarracina perched on a hill high above the sea, its Temple of Jupiter Anxur on the *Mons Neptunius* gleaming in the late afternoon sun. With every turn of the wheel, our cart was bringing us closer to Rome—and to a rendezvous with Paul. Would there be confrontation, or conciliation? I could hardly wait to find out.

When we arrived at the main inn of the town, a letter from Timothy was waiting for us, dispatched a day or two before. He was staying at the house of Rufus on the west bank of the Tiber opposite the Campus Martius section of Rome, a map and directions to which were enclosed. Relishing the thought of our journey's imminent end, Peter and I gave thanks for our safe passage thus far, and retired early. Despite the fatigue of the trip, I managed very little sleep, playing over in my mind the discussions of the past several days and wondering about what was yet to come.

Not in my wildest imagination could I have predicted what was in store for us.

Chapter 18

Peter woke me with a gentle shake and a smile. "It is time, Mark; let us pray, find some food, and ready the cart one last time. Rome awaits!" He bounced with a vigor that belied his age. We packed, watered the horse, paid for a hurried breakfast of dates and goat cheese with the few sesterces we had left, and departed the inn before the sun had a chance to heat the morning air.

On leaving Tarracina, the Appian Way stretched straight as an arrow across the flat Pontine Marshes, which in the summer heat are a haven for mosquitoes. A canal had been constructed parallel to the road, on which mule-drawn barges could carry passengers and freight between Rome and the sea. We soon overtook a pair of mules towing such a barge, and as they begrudgingly drifted to the side of the road to let us pass, my impatience showed, at least momentarily.

"Can't they move any faster? At this rate, it will be dark before we arrive at Rufus' house—if we have not been eaten alive by mosquitoes first!"

"Patience, Mark. Point your efforts toward the things you can control, and trust in God to handle the rest. Israel sojourned forty years in the desert before reaching the Promised Land; surely we can survive the trip through these marshes for a few hours longer. The time will pass quickly if we continue our discussions of the past few days."

"I am sorry, Peter; you are right. And there is one topic I would particularly like to hear you expound on further, while I still have you all to myself."

Peter smiled. "Let me guess: you want to explore the question of whether Jesus was truly the Son of God—in the literal rather than the adoptive sense of 'Son.' Is that it?"

"You have guessed correctly; but how did you know?"

"Well, we will soon be meeting up with Paul, whose views on that subject are well known—and as you have made no secret of your hope that he and I will reconcile, I surmised that you would be concerned about whether he and I disagree on such a transcendent topic. After all, if Jesus truly was God Himself in the flesh, it would change the focus of our faith, from what he said and did, to what he is."

"Indeed it would, Peter."

"But I am afraid that I have already told you what I know. In all the time I spent with him, I never once heard Jesus make such a claim. Given the method of his execution, I have to question whether he made such a claim to the Sanhedrin at his trial. His self-reference 'Son of Man' was ambiguous at best. There is much he did say which suggests that he did not believe himself to be divine: telling us he did not know when the end times would come because only God had such knowledge; telling James and John he had no authority to reserve places of honor in the kingdom for them because only God had that authority; and so on. Surely these statements give context to the proper interpretation of more ambiguous ones, such as his chiding the rich man for calling him 'good' when no one is good but God alone. He often prayed to God. And the great miracles he performed—control of the sea, exorcisms, cures of various physical afflictions, even raising someone from the dead—are not entirely without precedent in the Scriptures. The same is true of his bodily ascension into the heavens; Elijah was taken up in a similar way, as was Enoch."

"Yes, Peter, but what I want to know is, what do *you* believe? Despite all this, do you think Jesus was God—*is* God—or not?"

Peter's voice was firm. "I believe Jesus is the holiest, most divinely inspired and most God-like man who ever existed, the true Messiah, whose perfect unity of will with God in the divine plan of salvation has resulted in his being raised from the dead and exalted by God above all others, to the point even of being given power over all creation, and thus being worthy of worship and adoration. But was he God incarnate, the eternal Creator of the universe Himself in the cloak of human flesh? I have some difficulty with that notion. Surely any Jew must!"

"Paul is a Jew, and *he* does not."

Peter smiled in response. "And *you* are a Jew, Mark; what do *you* believe?"

"I don't know what to believe any more, Peter. I have no doubt that our Lord was filled completely with the spirit of God. But God-become-man is quite another thing. Through discussions with Timothy, I have lately been pondering the notion of our becoming aware of the mystical union between humanity and God; but we are talking now not of any mere indwelling of divine spirit—which every believer may have—but of a human being actually *being* God. I suppose I also have some difficulty understanding how, if God is One as we know He is, He could also be a man like us, a man with limitations on his knowledge that God could never have, a man who died as God could never die."

"And what is Paul's answer to that dilemma?"

"I suppose it is that upon the birth of Jesus—which according to Paul was to a virgin, as prophesied by Isaiah—he assumed a second nature, one of mortal flesh coexisting with his divine nature, certain elements of which he temporarily laid aside. Are you familiar with the ancient play by Euripides that is called *The Bacchae*?"

"No."

"Its opening verse has Dionysus, the son of Zeus, saying 'I have put off the god and taken human shape.' I suppose Paul's notion is similar."

"Perhaps that is where he got it. But what do *you* think of this concept?"

"I think that if God is truly One, it is a hard concept to grasp. If elements of the divine essence were put aside at his birth, then either Jesus was not simultaneously fully God and fully man, or the one God has split into two for the thirty-odd years that Jesus walked this earth."

"You wrestle with these concepts as a philosopher does, Mark! I am afraid I can give you very little help here. My notions of what it means for God to be One are the simple product of revelation in the

Scriptures, not those of Parmenides or the Pythagoreans. In matters of faith and doctrine on which Jesus has not spoken, my primary concern is not so much with whether a theory is logical, but with whether it is essential."

"What do you mean?"

"I ask myself whether the concept of the incarnation is essential to the gospel we proclaim, or whether, if Jesus be merely a mortal man who was exalted by God to a supreme status, that gospel will nevertheless retain its force and validity. We must, of course, first define each particular element of the gospel in order to answer this question. For example, we preach that Jesus sacrificed his life as atonement for the sin of mankind—and so I ask myself whether he of necessity had to be God incarnate in order for his death to achieve this."

"And what do you conclude?" I asked.

"That it is required only that Jesus have been sinless, *not* that he have been God. Surely only a sinless man, who nevertheless offers his life in sacrifice for sin, can achieve the perfection of sacrifice needed for the expiation of sin. But I cannot see any necessity to go further than this, and insist that his death could never have achieved that expiation unless he was divine as well."

"But wouldn't you agree that if God were to provide an ultimate sacrifice to demonstrate His unconditional love, there could be no greater sacrifice than the life of His only son?" I asked, thinking back to Timothy's observation on the point.

"Of course I would agree, Mark; but it does not follow that that is what must have happened. You presume that *God's* sacrifice is required for forgiveness of *man's* sin. Putting aside the questionable logic of such a requirement, why indulge a presumption at odds with our entire religious tradition, which focuses on *man's* sacrifice for his *own* sin? No, Mark; as I mentioned yesterday, I see what Jesus accomplished on that cross as a perfection of the sacrifice of *Yom HaKippurim*, the Day of Atonement when the high priest stands before God as a representative of Israel, with their names engraved on the jewels of his breastplate. He sacrifices an unblemished goat as a sin offering and brings its blood into the Holy of Holies where he sprinkles it as an intercession for God to forgive his people. Then he lays his hands on the head of a second goat while confessing the communal sins of Israel, and sends it out into the wilderness to die. But clearly such a sacrifice is vicarious rather than personal, and thus does not embody the love and obedience that true repentance demands. In contrast, Jesus' self-sacrifice achieves universal forgiveness of sin precisely by being personal, by demonstrating the ultimate love that is the antithesis of sin, the ultimate obedience that fulfills Israel's covenant. It is as representative and sin-bearer of mankind that his sacrifice has efficacy; and for this, his humanity rather than his divinity is key.

"And so it is in every aspect of the gospel we preach. Jesus' mission was to proclaim *God* as our heavenly Father, not to proclaim *himself* as divine. He was as truly God's representative to man as he was man's representative to God—but in neither manifestation is his deity required. I am not prepared to say that only the Son of God, incarnate into our nature, could qualify for such work."

"Paul would surely take issue with you, Peter."

"I know he would. And whether Paul's position is the product of reason or of revelation, I cannot say, although his letter to the Galatians suggests the latter. But if it is the product of reason, he is reasoning differently than I. Rather than deciding who Jesus is based on what he said and did, Paul's insistence on the divinity of Jesus is based on his view that such divinity is essential to a proper understanding of the meaning of the gospel. From the explanatory value of the incarnation to his theology, Paul concludes that the incarnation must be a historical fact. I cannot follow that logic; it seems to me to be reasoning the thing exactly backwards. Perhaps, in the end, Paul's view will prove to be the right one. But I myself cannot bear witness to any facts supporting that particular tenet, nor do I hold to it as a necessary conclusion."

Listening to Peter's three challenges to belief in Jesus' divinity—tension with Jewish monotheism, lack of clear evidence that Jesus made any such claim, and lack of necessity to the underlying message of salvation that he preached—I felt myself beginning to question the feelings of certainty I had when discussing these same matters with Timothy. I decided that I must grapple with the most fundamental objection first.

"I am not prepared to concede, Peter, that belief in Jesus' divinity would require abandoning our faith in one true God. Can there not be several manifestations of a single divine being?"

"Do you mean at the same time, or at different times?" Peter asked.

"Well, I suppose I mean at the same time, a single being with a dual nature; for if the human nature were not simultaneous with the divine, then we would be forced to conclude that Jesus was not truly God while he walked the earth, and as well that he is not truly human now."

"Neither one of those conclusions would offend me, Mark; but let me understand you further. Give me an example of what you mean by several manifestations of a single being."

I thought for a moment, and then replied. "An example might be water, which manifests itself as ice when very cold and as vapor when very hot. I consider it to be one substance, in various forms. Cannot the same be possible for God?"

"But your notion was that of *simultaneous* manifestations. Water is not liquid and ice at the same time, nor liquid and vapor at the same time. It changes from one to the other."

"Perhaps 'manifestations' is the wrong word, then. What I mean is a simultaneous dual nature, both God and man."

"Now you are speaking of two natures, two substances rather than two forms. But if Father and Son are distinct forms of a single divine substance, then they are not distinct natures at all; they are one nature—at least *now*, after the resurrection, when any temporary laying aside of the divine you posit has ceased. Is that what Paul teaches?"

"I am not sure," I responded after a considering the matter for a moment. I recalled Paul's writing to the Corinthians that at the end times, after all things were subjected to Jesus, Jesus would subject himself to God. Did Paul thus see a measure of inequality between the Father and the Son even *after* the resurrection, so as to preclude their being a single divine substance? Timothy's discussion of the concept of logical possibility—how even God could not make a square circle, because the definitions of both were mutually exclusive—came rushing back to me. In positing a simultaneous dual nature, was I stumbling over a definitional problem? Perhaps that was what was gnawing at me. These notions of divine substance and divine essence certainly needed to be defined more robustly before any conclusion could be drawn on whether they are mutually exclusive with the human substance, the human essence. How I wished that Timothy were sitting in the cart with us, explaining the *'isness'* of God to Peter as he had to me!

But Peter was not through. "Let us ask this simultaneous dual nature question a bit differently, Mark. As I understand it, Paul suggests that Jesus *always* was God and *became* a man, not that he was a man who became God, correct?"

"That is correct; for if he was man-become-God rather than God-become-man, we would be forced to conclude that Jesus was an *adopted* son of God rather than truly of God's eternal essence, truly equal to the Father."

"Nor would I find *that* conclusion offensive, Mark. Indeed, the notion of a truly sinless person, one whose love is so intense and perfect that he willingly gives his life in sacrifice and thereafter is anointed by God to a position of highest honor and achieves true union with God as an adoptive son, has some appeal to me. But let us explore further your contrary presumption of Jesus as God-become-man. How then are we to explain Jesus' interaction with God as a separate being, as when he prayed to the Father? What are we to make of his disclaiming knowledge reserved to the Father?"

"I suppose again, that we must view him as having temporarily laid aside his divinity."

"So," Peter said with a smile, "we are now abandoning the simultaneity you premised earlier?"

The fisherman had once again caught me in his net! "Peter, you are making my head spin! It is all very confusing."

"Indeed it is. But do not be troubled; there is no need to work out a perfectly logical theology here. We accept on faith the core tenet that God is One. Let us acknowledge that there are some mysteries we may never understand; but let us also be slow to make assumptions regarding the nature of Jesus which cloud our understanding of that core tenet. This is why I fall back on the simple principle that if an assumption is not essential to the gospel we preach, we ought not to preach that assumption as gospel."

"But this is precisely where you and Paul differ, Peter. He sees the divinity of our Lord as essential to the salvation wrought by the cross."

"Well then, we will agree to disagree," Peter said with a tone of finality. Unlike me, Peter was not concerned to seek a resolution of the disagreement. But in my own mind, I could not leave it alone. And as our cart rambled through the thickening countryside on the outskirts of Rome, I thought back to my discussion with Timothy of Jesus as juxtaposed with Adam, humbly relinquishing equality with God rather than grasping for it as Adam had.

Yet in pondering Peter's notion of a sinless man offering his life in atonement for the sins of mankind, I started to see a different symmetry between the Genesis story and the cross. Just as Satan, by tricking Adam into sin, had acquired the power of death over sinful man, so had Satan forfeited that power by himself falling victim to a divine deception, when through his agents he killed a man on whom he had no claim—the sinless Jesus of Nazareth. Perhaps there was something to this after all! I closed my eyes and began to imagine all sorts of variations on that theme.

Suddenly Peter grabbed my arm and jolted me back into reality. "Look there, Mark!" He pointed ahead of us. "What is . . . do you see it?!"

As my eyes focused on the hills of the great City spread out in the distance before us, I gasped in disbelief, and then in horror, at the thick black smoke, tinged with orange flame, billowing into the darkening skies ahead.

Rome was on fire!

Chapter 19

The blaze had started in a flat area between the Palatine and Caelian hills, spreading on the wind throughout the entire length of the valley, consuming level portions first, and then rising to the adjacent hills. In the twilight, as we struggled against the tide of humanity exiting the City through the wide archway of the Capenan Gate just to the east of the Circus Maximus, Peter and I could actually see the conflagration progressing, coming within half a mile of us.

Chaos reigned all about us. Amid the shouts of men desperately carrying what household possessions they could bear, the wailings of terror-stricken women shepherding their children, and the trumpets of the Roman *vigiles urbani*—the brigade of paid night watchmen and firefighters, warning the panicked citizens to clear a path for them—we pressed forward as best we could. Soon the crowds, mostly heading directly toward us or perpendicular to us from our right to our left, became so thick that we were forced to turn and find another route.

This was no time or place for a horse and cart, and looking into the eyes of the desperate refugees fleeing the City, I feared that at any moment we would be relieved of ours by force. My suggestion of proceeding on foot and dragging our trunks behind us was quickly dismissed by Peter. "Leaving the cart makes sense, but this horse is our best hope for getting through. Let us see if it can carry both of us as we try to find a passable route. We will take the parchments and whatever necessities we can easily carry, and leave the trunks with the cart."

I quickly opened the trunks and gathered up the parchments and what clothes I could hold in my arms, while Peter disconnected the cart and climbed onto the horse's back. It was obvious to us that we both could not ride, so I handed the parchments up to Peter and tucked the rest of our possessions under my arm and over my shoulders as I took the horse by its bridle and proceeded on foot. But even this proved to be no easy task as night fell and smoke drifted through the narrow streets. Unfamiliar with the City and unable to read the map, I took my best guess, and trusted that the crowds would also be heading towards the Tiber, away from the ominous orange glow that lit up ever more of the night sky with each passing minute.

We found ourselves swept along by the press of fleeing Romans, south toward the Aventine hill and thence west down to the river, which we were then able to follow north again, managing to skirt the fire all the way to the Campus Martius. The huge mass of people attempting to cross the Tiber at the Pons Aemilius was daunting, but with great effort we pressed through it, and once across the bridge we continued northward along the west bank of the river.

After several hours, we somehow managed to find Rufus' house on the corner of a narrow alley, the first of a dozen three story buildings cramped together. Rufus ran an olive oil shop with his brother Alexander on the first floor, and occupied the second floor with his family. The din of the crowds had subsided, and we yelled up to him—and Timothy's face appeared at the window. "God be praised; you found us! I'm coming down," he shouted, and disappeared into the house.

As we embraced at the front door, Timothy was more emotional than I had ever seen him. "My prayers have truly been answered, brothers! Come, we have much to discuss. This is Rufus; let him attend to the horse and your things. His wife will fix you something to eat, and you can wash the smell of smoke from your hair and change your clothes." We greeted Rufus with a thankful embrace, and followed Timothy into the house.

Soon we were seated at the table on the second floor, sharing some cheese and wine with Timothy and Rufus. "We should be safe from the flames here in the trans-Tiber," Rufus announced. "The wind has eased somewhat, and it is blowing toward the fire. But there is another danger to be reckoned with." He glanced furtively at Timothy.

"It is Paul," Timothy explained. "A contingent of his accusers arrived a week ago from Asia, and his trial before the Emperor is set to commence—although this fire will undoubtedly delay it for a little while at least. But his accusers have caught the ear of Tigellinus, convincing him of Paul's guilt as the leader of a divisive and seditious sect that advocates lawlessness. The word we have heard from some of the brethren in Nero's household is that Tigellinus intends to see to it that Paul's trial ends in a sentence of death. We fear the rumor is true; Paul has just been removed from the quarters where he was under house arrest, to the Mamertine *carcer*, the prison at the Forum where condemned men are often held before execution."

"We have scheduled a meeting of the faithful for tomorrow night, in our secret place, to discuss what to do," Rufus added. "You must come. When Timothy announced that the great Simon Peter was on his way to Rome, the news spread among the believers faster than this fire. All of us are expecting you. There are thousands of believers in the City. Hopes are high that you will address the assembly—presuming that the meeting still takes place. But with this conflagration raging . . ."

Despite his evident fatigue, Peter did not hesitate. "I will be pleased to speak to the group, of course, although I may require a translator if Latin is in order. But I would prefer to see Paul first. Will that be possible, do you suppose?"

"It may depend on whether the blaze has been brought under control," Timothy offered. "If it has, I will take you to him in the morning; I know he is anxious to see you as well, and hopefully he is still being allowed visitors. But now you should sleep, both of you. Rufus and I will take turns staying awake, and rouse you if the fire spreads this way. Let us pray that it is extinguished without greater loss of life."

Timothy led us in a quick prayer, and then rose from the table, clasping his hand on my shoulder. Although bone-weary from the trip, I was too keyed up to sleep. "Go ahead and retire, Peter," I urged. "I will join you soon." Peter nodded and got up, too tired to protest.

As he followed Rufus into a back room, I motioned Timothy to stay, and he obliged me by sitting again.

"Rufus said there was a 'secret place' for meetings, Timothy," I whispered. "Why the need for secrecy? What is going on?"

"Rufus can tell you more than I, but evidently these are dangerous times to profess allegiance to Christ too openly," he replied. "Rumors have been circulating about the Way—that we are a dangerous and perverse cult, urging Romans to reject their gods and their emperor, and engaging in all manner of abhorrent practices at our gatherings, even including human sacrifice and cannibalism. No one knows the source of these rumors, although Paul has his suspicions. But there have already been some arrests, some accusations, even a resolution introduced in the Senate—and fear is in the air. The faithful have been keeping a low profile for months now. Paul's trial could not have come at a more inopportune time."

"Nor could this fire," Rufus added upon entering the room. "If a scapegoat must be found, surely we are among the groups that might be blamed. But tomorrow will be time enough to concern ourselves with such things, my friends. Come, Mark, let me show you to your bed."

I said good night to Timothy and dutifully followed Rufus into the back room, where Peter was already snoring and a second cot was made up and waiting for me. Still unprepared to sleep, I asked Rufus to join me in prayer. We knelt against the cot and prayed in low voices, I in thanks for Rufus and his family, he in thanks for God's having brought Peter and me safely to Rome. Then we sat on the cot for a few moments just watching Peter sleep, while a faint scent of smoke wafted through the open window on the night air that flickered the candle flame.

"Rufus," I inquired at length, "are things really that bad for the faithful here in the City? And are we putting you and your family at risk if we stay here?"

"These are tense times for the faithful, to be sure," he replied softly. "But do not be troubled for us. Anything that my wife and I may be privileged to do for this blessed man sleeping before us, the Lord's own trusted friend and apostle, we count as a great honor to do. I would risk much for such an honor." It was plain to see that Rufus was a man of solid faith. I knew that he and his mother had befriended Paul many years earlier in Antioch, and I could not restrain myself from asking him how he had come to believe.

"Ever since I can remember, Mark, the name of Jesus of Nazareth was revered in my household. My father actually met him—in a manner of speaking. Incredible though it may sound, he helped carry Jesus' cross on the day of his crucifixion! When you are not so tired, I must tell you the story he related to me."

Fascinated, I begged Rufus to tell me the story at once. He let out a sigh, and in a low voice began:

"My father, whose name was Simon, was a devout Jew from Cyrene. When I was a baby and my brother still in the womb, we traveled to Jerusalem to worship for the Passover, staying with some friends in Bezetha just to the north of the city. On the morning of the Passover, my father was walking down through the fields toward the city on his way to worship at the Temple, when he encountered a group of Roman soldiers leading three men carrying crosses out of the city, on their way to be crucified. Following close behind were some of the chief priests and scribes. One of the condemned men, wearing a crown on his head fashioned from thorns, stumbled and fell under the weight of his cross. The centurion in charge ordered my father: 'You, there! Help this criminal with his cross!" Glancing at the priests and the scribes, my father protested that it was forbidden to do any work on Passover, but the centurion threatened him with a similar fate if he disobeyed. So he lifted the crossbeam onto his broad shoulders and carried it the rest of the way, up the ridge along the main road, to a hill known as Golgotha.

"When the spot was reached, he set the beam down and watched as the soldiers tried to give Jesus some wine drugged with myrrh; but Jesus refused it. Then they stripped him of his garments and rolled dice for them. Finally they laid him down, stretched his arms and legs onto the cross and crucified him, and the two others as well, one on either side of him. On each cross they nailed a sign indicating the victim's name and the offense of which he had been convicted. Over Jesus' head the soldiers affixed a sign proclaiming 'The King of the Jews.'

"Throughout the morning passers-by derided him, saying things like 'So you were going to destroy the temple and rebuild it in three days! Save yourself now, by coming down from that cross!' The chief priests and scribes likewise insulted him, saying 'He saved others but cannot save himself! Let this Messiah, this King of Israel, come down from the cross now; if we see it, we will believe in him!' Even the criminals crucified with him taunted him. But he made no answer.

"My father was transfixed by the scene; he stayed and watched the suffering for hours. Crucifixion as a form of ultimate torture is evilly ingenious; the pain caused by full body weight hanging from the spikes in the wrists is excruciating, and instinctively forces the victim to push himself up slightly with his legs, which in turn increases the weight pressing against the spike through his feet until it, too, becomes a center of unbearable pain, causing the victim to allow his torso to sag once again from the wrists—and start the cycle again. The victim is thus constantly writhing in an exhausting and futile effort to find the least painful position, until all the muscles in his legs and arms are in uncontrollable spasms, adding to the agony caused by the spikes. When he finally tires to the point that he can barely avoid allowing all his weight to sag, he finds himself unable to breathe without pushing or pulling himself up slightly, presenting him the cruel choice between suffocating and increasing the already intolerable pain even more. Instinctively he chooses breathing, and thus greater torment, as long as he can.

"Around noon the skies grew dark, and remained that way until mid-day. Then suddenly my father heard Jesus cry out, *'Eloi, Eloi, lama sabachthani?'*—quoting the Psalm in Aramaic. Some of the bystanders thought he was calling on Elijah; one of them ran off to soak a sponge with sour wine, and stuck it on a reed to lift it to Jesus' lips, saying 'Now let us see if Elijah comes to his aid.' But Jesus could not drink. He uttered a final loud cry, and breathed his last.

"As soon as he died, an eerie silence befell the onlookers, my father included. All were still and somber, even the soldiers. The centurion said something in Latin, and bowed his head as if in reverence. Somehow everyone realized that they had killed an innocent man. And then," Rufus concluded, "my father turned and went on his way, forever changed by what he had seen."

For a few moments, Rufus and I just sat silently on the cot, until I broke the silence by thanking him for his story. He smiled weakly, wished me a good night and left the room quietly, as I stretched out on my bed to try to sleep.

But sleep would not come easily. I thought of the Psalmist's lament, *"They have pierced my hands and my feet; I can count all my bones. They look on and gloat over me; they divide my garments among them, and for my clothing they cast lots."* How prophetic! Extending my arms into the semi-darkness, I tried to imagine the feel of nails being driven into my wrists and feet, but quickly recoiled with a shudder, and curled myself into a fetal position. The unimaginable horror and brutality of death on the cross was overwhelming. In the face of such obvious agony as Jesus must have endured, mockery and derision by the bystanders, and especially by the priests and scribes, seemed outrageously inhumane. How could they have hated him so much?

My thoughts quickly turned to the Romans of today. Was a similar hatred of Jesus rearing its head again, directed now toward his followers? Could it have similar results?

In the dim candlelight I noticed the parchments lying on the floor next to Peter's bed. Quietly I gathered them up, spread them on my cot and strained my eyes to find the passage that I felt compelled to read. There it was:

> *'If anyone wishes to follow me, he must deny himself, take up his cross and follow in my steps. Whoever would save his life will lose it, but whoever loses his life for my sake and the gospel's will save it.'*

As I placed the parchments back on the floor by Peter's bed, the faint smell of smoke in the room took on a new significance for me. Timothy had said it right; fear was in the air. *My* fear.

I recalled what Peter had told me about Jesus' admonishment to his disciples at Gethsemani on the night of his arrest, and I prayed mightily that I, too, would not be put to the test.

Chapter 20

Despite being dotted with impressive monuments of marble and stone, much of Rome was a tinderbox of cramped and poorly constructed wooden tenements and apartment blocks, housing the city's plebian class like rabbits in a warren. With these squalid structures serving as a perfect fuel, the fire had intensified overnight, jumping from roof to roof. It had spread almost to Nero's palace on the Palatine, and was nearing the Forum and the adjacent temples.

All efforts to douse the flames with water, whether from the river or from the holding tanks, public baths and fountains fed by Rome's system of aqueducts, came to naught. The creation of strategic downwind firebreaks by tearing down and clearing wooden buildings in the fire's path had some limited success in places, but the blaze seemed to have a devious mind of its own, and with the changing wind as a coconspirator it found a way to circumvent virtually all human defenses. It would be several days before the fire would be controlled, longer until it would be fully extinguished.

Although not itself consumed by the flames, the Forum prison at the northeastern foot of the Capitoline Hill was close enough to the burn line to have required evacuation, as Peter, Timothy and I discovered when we arrived in the morning to try to visit Paul. Despite the chaos all around, we finally managed to learn where they had moved him, and set out for his new quarters of confinement adjacent to the Praetorian Guard barracks about a mile to the northeast, through the Viminal Gate just outside the walls of the city and, thankfully, away from the flames that were still ravaging Rome behind us.

Uncertain of Paul's new living arrangements and concerned about the fire, we had decided that it would be too risky to bring the parchments with us, and we left them in Rufus' care. I doubted that Paul would even ask about them; the meeting with Peter would surely overshadow everything else for him. As we made our way up the Quirinal Hill, I wondered whether their reunion would end up being contentious. The Paul I knew was both dogmatic to a fault and paranoid of perceived rivals—and learning that Peter's first order of business would be to address the believers might well fuel that paranoia. If he viewed Peter's trip to Rome as a challenge to his teachings or a threat to his position among the Roman faithful, Paul might well try to engage Peter in debate. The part of me that would have been thrilled to hear such a debate gave way to the common sense awareness that this was not the proper time. I hoped that Timothy would be able to diffuse the situation if it arose. I knew that *I* could not.

When we arrived at the camp, Timothy's fluent Latin proved to be a boon; we were soon directed to the building containing Paul's cell. We had no trouble at all persuading the guard outside, who had been assigned to Paul since his arrival in Rome and had developed a great fondness and respect for Paul, to allow us a visit. Timothy followed him inside first, Peter and I close behind him, down a narrow and dimly lit corridor. The guard unlocked a large iron door and swung it open, motioning us to enter the small vaulted chamber.

The diminutive man in the tattered tunic rising out of the lone chair to meet us was barely recognizable as the great Apostle to the Gentiles that I knew. He seemed to have aged ten years since I last saw him, thinner and paler, now completely bald, but with a long grey beard. A skin disease that had flared up from time to time since his youth now completely covered one side of his face, and cataracts had begun to cloud his eyes. But his voice was every bit as firm and forceful as I remembered.

"Praise be to God, Timothy; you have brought Mark—and *Peter*! Welcome to my humble abode, brothers!" Paul embraced me first, and Peter in turn. "I regret that I can offer you neither seats nor refreshment, but as you see, the accommodations for this new palace of mine are still being worked out. Indeed, Luke, my dear companion, has just gone off in search of another chair; you must have just missed him. I trust that the journey has treated you well?"

Peter spoke first. "Quite well, thanks be to God. It is good to see you again, Paul. You have been often in my prayers."

"And you in mine," Paul replied, not as convincingly. "Imagine my surprise when Timothy informed me that he and Mark had met up with you in Tarentum, and that you were on your way here. So august an emissary from the church in Jerusalem suggests an important mission indeed! Tell me, Peter; what doctrinal disturbance brings you to Rome? Surely you have not come all this way simply to pay me a social visit!"

Peter was taken aback by the bluntness of Paul's question, and by how quickly the perfunctory pleasantries had ended. "Doctrinal disturbance? You waste no time at all, *do* you, Paul?"

"I have none to waste. No doubt Timothy has told you that my trial is imminent."

"He has. Are you concerned that I might have come in order to testify against you?"

"Well, the timing is rather coincidental, don't you think?"

While I was too mesmerized by the sparring of these two Titans to say anything, Timothy did not like where the conversation was going, and quickly interjected a bit of diplomacy. "I am heartened to see that you have maintained your sense of humor, Paul! Please, sit down; we have some pressing business to discuss. There is to be a meeting of the faithful tonight to talk about your trial." Timothy shot a furtive glance at Peter. "The crowd is expecting Peter to speak, and he has come to seek your counsel first."

Recognizing Paul's sensitivity to any effort, real or perceived, to challenge his authority, Peter took Timothy's cue. "Indeed, Paul. Though neither one of us founded the church in this City, I am sure that your time here has given you the pulse of the community. I thought I would seek the benefit of your perspectives before addressing the congregation tonight, and perhaps even deliver a personal message from you."

Whether he accepted Peter's explanation at face value or not, Paul appeared to be sufficiently mollified by this olive branch that his tone immediately dropped its undertones of conflict and sarcasm—although I was left with the suspicion that he was consciously changing his tone in order to make the most of an opportunity to dissuade Peter from any Judaizing inclinations Peter might have.

"My perspective is that Gentile converts, who make up the majority of Roman believers, are not much different from Gentile converts in Greece and Asia. They are unsatisfied with pagan doctrines and pagan idols whose worship brings them no solace. They are hungry for the gospel's message of grace and forgiveness, drawn to its promise of immortality and the life of charity it fosters. But they resist any notion that they should follow Jewish law or practices, more so than in any of the other churches. Ever since Claudius banished the Jews from Rome fifteen years ago, they have been inclined of necessity to indentify themselves as separate from the Jews—and that has remained part of their mindset despite the Jews' return after Claudius' death.

"For their part, the Jewish-Christians in Rome are not ardent Torah observers; what practices they cling to are largely in private, as there is still some residual anti-Jewish sentiment in the city. The Jews, in turn, blame Christians for the Claudian expulsion, since the riots in the synagogues that sparked his edict were themselves a result of missionary efforts to preach Christ to the Jews. Their resentment against Jewish-Christians, whom they view as traitors, has been slow to dissipate. Indeed, even among the believers themselves there is still some Jewish-Gentile tension.

"The religion of the common Roman is rather naïve, devoid of most philosophical reflection. Their worship is largely a cultural phenomenon. Those who believe in the gods as more than myths worship in their temples to court their favor or avoid their displeasure, while those who believe that only clouds crown Mount Olympus nevertheless worship along side them simply to avoid the appearance of atheism. In neither case do they hold any notion of a loving, personal relationship with the gods, and they view advocates of that notion with suspicion. Roman pagans have lately come to view us as indulging in a dangerous superstition, akin to many that have beset Rome in the past. This has further divided Christians from Jews, who for their own protection now desire even more to separate themselves from any association with Christians. Jewish-Christians in the city thus feel isolation from both sides.

"So you see, Peter, matters here are somewhat complicated by politics and by history. But the gospel I have preached to the Romans is unifying rather than divisive. And that is how it should remain, wouldn't you agree?"

"I would indeed. You must set your mind at ease, Paul. I have no intention of stirring any dissention among the faithful. To the contrary, anything I can do to strengthen their faith . . ."

We heard the bolt of the door, and turned as it swung open. There stood Luke, a chair in his arms and a look of surprise in his eyes. I had met Luke once before, on my last trip to Rome, and recognized him at once.

"Come in, Luke!" Paul called to him. "Our dear friends have come for a visit, as you see. You remember Mark, of course—and this fine specimen is none other than Simon Peter."

"Peace be with you," Luke said as he put down the chair and embraced us, the door slamming behind him. His voice was laced with apprehension. "Peter, I am greatly honored to meet you! Ever since Timothy told us a few days ago that you were coming, I have been looking forward to this day. But now, I am afraid that your visit was ill-timed. And indeed, you must leave at once! You may be in danger if you stay here."

"What kind of danger?" Peter demanded.

"The gravest kind. I just overheard the guards outside speaking. Tigellinus is on his way here to question Paul. Right now!"

Peter was unmoved. "Why should that be of concern to me?"

"What if he knows of your arrival in Rome?" Luke replied. "He may draw a connection between your visit and the fire."

"That possibility is not as unlikely as it may sound, Peter," Timothy added. "The entire community of believers has been abuzz with the news I brought that you were coming, and word could easily have leaked to the Praetorian. The two events might well strike Tigellinus as a bit too coincidental."

"Luke and Timothy are right," Paul chimed in. "You should leave at once. There is no need to take any chances with this dangerous man."

Before Peter could protest, we heard the clanking of approaching soldiers in the hall, and then once again the sound of the bolt being flung back. I held my breath as the door was thrust open by one of the guards, who then stiffened straight up, stood aside and announced "Make way for the Prefect!"

Wearing segmented armor as if preparing for battle, Tigellinus entered, scowled quickly at each of us, and then fixed his eyes on Paul. His lips curled into a slight smile and his eyes narrowed, as he spoke in perfect Greek, right down to the undertone of sarcasm. "Paul of Tarsus! How nice to see you again!"

"And you, Prefect," Paul replied in kind, his eyes fearless and defiant. "To what do I owe this honor?"

"The only honor to be bestowed on you is the honor of a fair trial before Caesar, followed by an honorable death befitting a Roman citizen, as you claim you are. Otherwise, I would simply have left you at the *carcer*, where by now you might have been consumed by the flames. Perhaps that would have been true justice, as I have little doubt that your followers are responsible in some way for this accursed fire. Truthfully, what better diversion to postpone your trial could they possibly have devised?"

Paul, who had written to the Romans years earlier that they should respect and obey the authorities, was indignant at this accusation. "If by '*my* followers' you mean the peace loving, law abiding and gentle followers of Jesus Christ, the Son of the one true God, you are surely mistaken."

"Am I? And would I also be mistaken that the first and most respected disciple of this Christ, a Galilean named Simon Peter, just happens to have arrived in Rome on the very day that this fire was started?"

Paul made no answer, except by the pale look on his face. Indeed, except for Peter's, all of our faces were instantly drained of color, which caused Tigellinus to smile a bit more widely. "Come now, Paul; surely you did not think me ignorant of such goings-on! Caesar has spies in every quarter of the city, even among your faithful flock of religious fanatics."

"What need have you to question me, then?" Paul retorted.

"It is this Simon Peter whom I wish to question, and I suspect you know where he can be found. Or, perhaps one of your friends here would be so kind as to reveal his whereabouts—under torture only if necessary, of course."

Peter stood tall and took a step toward Tigellinus. "That will not be necessary, Prefect. I am the man you seek."

Chapter 21

It was not Peter's arrest but the fire, still blazing in many parts of the City, that postponed the secret meeting of the faithful that evening. Back at Rufus' house, Timothy and I did our best to put aside the emotion and confusion of the day, and discussed options for moving the parchments in the event that the fire spread too close. Rufus had spent most of the day on the front lines of the fire fighting brigade at the edge of the Campus Martius; his assessment was that the flames would likely be contained before they could overcome the buffer of the river and threaten his house. While we prayed that he was right, the safest course, we decided, would be to entrust the parchments to one of the brethren living further west of the Tiber if the flames drew any nearer.

Luke had promised us he would find out where Peter was being held and report back as soon as he could, but as dusk turned to darkness without his arrival we began to fear for his safety as well. In his search he might easily have found himself cut off or trapped by the flames in some dark quarter of the city. A physician by training, Luke was just the type to stop and render aid to anyone in need regardless of risk to himself.

Gazing out the window at the eerie orange glow in the night sky, I wondered aloud whether the fire had been sent by God to destroy Rome for its wickedness—and how many good people would lose their lives or fortunes in it as well. "That was ever His way, at least as recorded in Scripture," I said to Timothy. "Whenever His wrath flared against a people, God destroyed the innocent with the guilty. This fire may do the same."

Timothy had an answer at the ready. "Why should you blame the conflagration on God? Cannot man, whether through intent or carelessness, be responsible for this calamity?"

"Responsible for the initial spark, perhaps. But whether God actively caused the fire, or passively allows it to continue despite having the power to stop it, makes no difference to the innocent. Its effects on them are the same."

"The effects may be the same, but not the moral culpability. Permit me to ask you a question, Mark. Which of these two is the more blameworthy: the soldier who swings a sword at an innocent child, or the general who fails to stay the soldier's arm?"

"Provided he was under no compulsion, the soldier is the more blameworthy. He made a free choice, with knowledge of its evil consequences and without intent to further any greater good—which is the very essence of immorality."

"Very well. And what of the general who failed to prevent the evil?"

"His guilt is less, but as he has complete power over those under his command and could have prevented it, he should bear some measure of responsibility for it. If the general had restrained the soldier, even bound his arm such that he could not swing his sword, the sword would not have struck the innocent child."

"But a soldier who cannot wield his sword is of no use to the general; it would be counterproductive so to disable the soldier from doing harm."

"That is true."

"What, then, is the general's responsibility?"

"For his part, the general is morally obliged to order his soldiers not to smite an innocent child, and to punish them if they choose to disobey."

"Indeed; but having given that command and having threatened to punish those who break it, are we agreed that he must still allow his soldiers freedom of motion and freedom of choice, simply in order to have a functioning military?"

"Yes, I will concede that soldiers must remain free to wield their swords. But I do not see the analogy, Timothy. Unlike the general, God has the power not only to prevent an occurrence, but to ameliorate its effects. If the general could somehow magically protect a struck child from the effects of the blow, so that neither pain nor disfigurement nor death resulted, surely he would be morally obliged to exercise that power."

"And if he did so, the soldiers would quickly come to realize that the natural consequences of their actions had been altered, such that no true evil ensues from their striking an innocent child; is that not so?"

"Yes."

"Then they would no longer have the same capacity to be moral actors in respect to the child, would they?"

"Explain."

"As you stated, the essence of immorality embraces making a free choice with knowledge of its evil consequences—and if, through the general's magical after-the-fact intervention, the soldiers know that their actions will have no such evil consequences, their choice can no longer be moral or immoral."

"I see your point."

"In like manner, if God chooses not to stop the suffering that mankind has put in motion, it is because depriving human actions of their natural consequences also deprives humanity of any meaningful freedom of choice, any real possibility of being moral actors."

"I suppose that is so. But is our capacity to be moral actors so important as to justify the misery that our actions often inflict on others?"

"I am not qualified to judge what is and is not of greatest importance in the divine plan, Mark. What I can say is this: but for our capacity to be moral actors, we would not enjoy free will at all. And without free will, we could not serve His purpose for us. It is to the greater glory of God that we are called to exercise our will for good rather than evil, to choose love rather than hate—just as the Lord taught us."

"You make a convincing argument for God's allowing the natural consequences of human actions to run their course, Timothy. But what of the suffering of innocent people caused by illness, floods, plagues, famines and the like? Why does God allow such evils?"

"Do you mean, why does God allow the suffering that results from these things; or why does He allow the things themselves to occur?"

"What would be the difference?"

"A most important one, given the value of moral choice by beings with free will. God could not eliminate our capacity to experience the ill effects of these disasters without also eliminating all capacity for moral choice. For if God had created a world in which pain and suffering were entirely eliminated, no man could do harm to another, since his victim would be unable to suffer injury; nor could any man do good to his neighbor, who would have no needs to be fulfilled."

"I appreciate the distinction. Then I ask, why does God allow these calamities themselves to occur as part of the natural world?"

"It is a difficult question. The miseries of sickness or natural disasters afflict the just and the unjust alike, so it is difficult to view them as punishment for sin unless we posit some original sin by some ancient ancestor that continues to taint us all. And indeed, many stories and myths have come down to us, attempts to explain an unsatisfactory part of God's creation by setting up a morally culpable scapegoat, usually female, whether we call her Eve, or Lilith, or Pandora. But such myths do not answer the question of why their moral culpability should be visited upon us; punishment for the sins of some distant forefather seems unjust. Many find it more palatable to declare that natural evils are simply the work of Satan."

"If Satan is the cause, and God allows Satan to have such reign over the natural world, the explanation is equally unsatisfactory."

"Is it? Cannot Satan also possess and act upon a free will opposed to God, just as humans can? And cannot the exercise of that free will cause pain and suffering, just as the exercise of human free will can?"

"No doubt that is possible; but if God allows the adverse consequences of Satanic free will for the same reason as He allows them in the case of human free will, it would follow that Satan must have the same capacity as we to be a moral actor, the same the ability to choose good over evil—and likewise, that God prizes this capacity so highly as to outweigh the human pain and suffering entailed by Satan's malevolent choices. That does not fit with my notion of Satan as a being who is invariably malevolent by nature."

"Nor with mine; but who is to say that God's reasons are the same in each case? The alternative is to reject the existence of Satan as a being of free will altogether and turn the concept of Satan simply into a personification of all the evils in the world that are otherwise unexplained—or else to acknowledge that Satan exists, but with powers that are limited to the influencing of human choice."

"Neither of which, of course, brings us any closer to an explanation of why God permits the suffering that follows illness and natural disasters."

"Whether or not we ascribe illnesses and natural calamities to Satan, perhaps God allows them to strike the innocent simply to humble us, just as He did with Job. And as with Job, our questioning of God's justice in permitting such afflictions comes to this: that His ways are beyond our comprehension. But let us not be too harsh on our Creator. It is enough that He has sent His Son, Christ Jesus, to rectify our sins and to guide us along the path of righteousness, without expecting an immediate end to all naturally caused sufferings as well."

"But why should we not expect this? Jesus surely has power over the forces which produce sickness, for he healed many; and also power over the natural world, for it likewise obeyed his commands. Peter has been relating many such examples to me. And Paul teaches that our Lord's death on the cross conquered all the forces of evil; does he not?"

"Indeed he does, Mark."

"Then I do not understand. Paul insists that our Lord conquered sin; yet we sin. He says that our Lord conquered death; yet we die. He wrote to the Colossians that the principalities and powers of the world have been disarmed by the cross, and led off as captives in a public display of triumph—yet we continue to be plagued by evils of every kind. Where is that triumphal procession?"

"You presume that all naturally caused sufferings are the doings of the devil. That is not my view. Jesus' work was redemptive, which is to say that he conquered sin. That victory over sin is a present one, for though sin is yet with us, we now have been given the power to overcome it in our own lives. Similarly his victory over death, though death is yet with us, offers a resurrection and eternal life. But it is otherwise with natural calamities. These ills are yet with us and we have no power to stop them. Therefore, we must either abandon the notion of Jesus as the present liberator of mankind from all forces of evil, or—as I suggest we do—abandon the notion that Satanic forces are responsible for natural tragedies."

"If we do as you suggest—if we distinguish moral evils from physical evils, consigning only the former to voluntary acts, demonic or human, and the latter to the involuntary workings of the natural world—then God as the Creator of the natural world is responsible for much pain and suffering that could have been avoided if the constitution of things had been otherwise ordered. Are we not then left with the conclusion that God Himself is a force of evil?"

"Not at all, Mark. There are two necessary premises to your conclusion: that all pain and suffering is necessarily evil, and that God could have otherwise ordered the constitution of things to avoid physical evil without sacrifice of either life itself or the possibility of moral choice. I am prepared to challenge either one of those premises, or at least to show that they are mutually exclusive."

"Please do."

"First, we have already agreed that human beings must be capable of experiencing physical pain, hunger, cold, even blindness and physical infirmities of various kinds—in short, all of the miseries that one person can inflict on another—for our capacity to experience them is a necessary predicate to the existence of moral choice. Therefore, these things are not evil in themselves; the question is one of degree, of how much suffering should be permitted by God."

"That is fair."

"And in order to sense pain, hunger, cold and the rest, our physical bodies must be adapted in relation to the physical world, whose rough edges, so to speak, provide the impetus to affect our bodies in these uncomfortable and even devastating ways; is it not so?"

"It is."

"Our freedom to use those rough edges to advantage, even if pain sometimes results from our doing so, is a good and necessary thing. For example, consider the edges of your own teeth; you would never be able to chew your food without also having the ability to bite your lip on occasion. The only alternative would be to surrender the freedom to work your jaw muscles—and very quickly you would perish, would you not?"

"That is true."

"In like manner, is it not fair to presume that all of these rough edges are a natural part of the wider cosmos which embodies the physical conditions necessary for human life to be sustained in the first place?"

"I suppose so."

"Now suppose that God, instead of tailoring the natural laws of the cosmos to favor the sustenance of life, were to reorder the world so as to smooth all of its rough edges on which man may be impaled, thereby eliminating anything that could cause human suffering. Would not the physical conditions necessary to sustain life be impacted?"

"That seems logical."

"But let us go further. Suppose God were to eliminate all those rough edges which have the capacity to produce physical ills, and simultaneously counteract the natural result of His reordering the natural world so as to preserve our physical existence. How, then, could any suffering arise through the acts and choices of man, who would have neither the rough edges of the physical world at his disposal as tools to inflict suffering on his fellow man, nor the experience of suffering even to know that such infliction is possible?"

"Again, I see your point. It seems, though, that everything comes back to enabling moral choice by mankind as the underlying explanation for God's allowing so much pain and suffering in the world, causing such misery to so many innocents. How can that be just? What of His moral choice?"

"Well, let us come back to your own definition of immorality—the exercise of free choice with knowledge of its evil consequences and without intent to further any greater good. If we apply the same test to God, and ascribe to Him an intention to further our capacity to be moral actors as a greater good, then you must admit that He passes the test!"

"Yes, provided that our capacity for moral choice is a greater good. But for it to come at such a price, I have to wonder."

Timothy's mouth curled in a smile as he answered me. "To question the wisdom of God's assessment is foolishness. We do not have the same knowledge of good and evil as God—and thankfully so. Do not wish to eat of the forbidden fruit of that tree!"

I could only smile in response. Timothy had developed a comfort with mankind's limited understanding of God's plan, a comfort that I could not seem to find. Yet there was something attractive in his calm acceptance of God's ways, something which made me want to follow his example of faith. The faith of true believers is infectious; it can inspire others even to great sacrifice, as I was about to learn in the ensuing days.

Chapter 22

Luke arrived early the next morning, safe from harm. Through persistence he had discovered Peter's detention site yesterday afternoon, but was not allowed in to visit him. Sensing something in the guards' reaction to him, Luke decided against coming directly to us for fear that he himself may have escaped arrest only for the purpose of leading Tigellinus' soldiers to Peter's cohorts. Instead, he had spent the night alone at his own quarters, and left in stealth before the sun was up. "I am confident that if I had a tail, it did not follow me here," he assured us. "But I think it would be unwise to attempt to visit Peter this morning. No doubt he is being interrogated further today." What manner of "interrogation" his captors might be employing, I did not want to imagine.

The fire had advanced but slightly during the night, not close enough to require us to evacuate. We decided to leave the parchments at Rufus' house, and made our way once again to see Paul. My thoughts, however, were of Peter. He and Paul had spent only a few minutes together yesterday, and neither the reconciliation I'd hoped for nor the confrontation I'd feared had had a chance to develop. Although these two pillars of the faith were finally in proximity in the same city, it was not at all certain that they would be given the chance to meet again—and ironically, it was Peter who now appeared to be the one most at risk.

We found Paul as we had left him, in good spirits despite his evident frailty. He mustered the strength to greet us warmly, and immediately inquired about Peter. "Do we know where he is being kept?" Paul asked in a tone of genuine concern.

"Yes," Luke replied, "not far from here. He is not being allowed visitors, at least as of yesterday. Perhaps Pomponia can arrange us access." Pomponia Graecina, as I would come to learn, was the wife of the respected Roman nobleman and war-hero Aulus Plautius, and a convert to the Way.

"An excellent suggestion, Luke! If she is still in Rome despite the fire, find her and try to gain an audience with her. Go now, and take Timothy with you. Mark will stay with me; we have some things to discuss."

As Luke and Timothy made their exit, I felt a tingling of excitement, sensing that I was finally about to learn the true reason Paul had called me to Rome. I pulled my chair close to Paul's, studying his face, waiting for him to begin. Once more I was struck by how much Paul seemed to have aged. But although his body was failing, there was still fire in the belly, still passion for the cause of Christ that drove this man and awed those around him into reverence.

"Thanks be to God for seeing you safely to Rome," Paul began. "I asked Timothy to bring you in the hope that you could assist me with some writing I had planned to do—an exposition on the import of our Lord's sayings as recorded in the parchments, lest they be misinterpreted or perverted by those who would stray from the fundamental truth that man has been reconciled to God through His Son. I thought you would be the perfect choice for such a task. You are quite familiar with the parchments, and a fine writer besides, with a style I could not hope to match even if my eyesight were not failing. But now, Mark, I must accept that there will not be enough time for such an enterprise. Rome is burning, and with it burns the candle of my remaining life in the flesh. We must find another way to make productive what is left of our time together."

I made no protest at Paul's suggestion of his impending death; it seemed palpably real, more so because of his resignation to it than anything else. I knew that Paul did not view his death as a negative in any respect; to the contrary, he was looking forward to it, while still remaining devoted to his life's work as long as that life continued. That Paul was willing to include me in his few remaining days was not only a great honor; it was my chance to make amends for having let him down in the past.

Still, my excitement at the prospect of lending myself to his service once more was laced with apprehension over what his notion of "productive" time with me might entail. Somehow I suspected that it might involve Peter. "Forgive me, Paul, but your brief confrontation with Peter yesterday has weighed heavily on my mind, and so I must ask you. Do you count Peter among those who stray from the truth of the gospel?"

Paul paused and sighed heavily before responding. "Not intentionally, perhaps, but there have been times when he has failed to appreciate how deeply the gospel alters relations between God and Israel, and I fear he has led others astray as a result. In Peter's case, even slight errors are magnified by virtue of his stature in the church. Quite naturally, Peter sees everything through Jewish eyes, and this colors his perception. The grace that has enabled me to overcome that natural impediment to a more global view of the gospel does not seem to have been given in equal measure to him—at least, not to the Peter I knew. But perhaps he has changed his views over the years. You have just spent most of the past two weeks with him; is he as solicitous of the Law as ever?"

"I am not fit to judge the extent of his solicitousness, Paul. No doubt it is safe to say that you and he do not agree on every detail of the Way. But is agreement on every aspect of the faith necessary? After all, Judaism has survived for centuries despite constant debate among its rabbis and teachers as to the requirements of the Law, and allegiance to differing camps has not shaken its fundamental core."

"You forget that as followers of Christ, we do not have the history, the tradition, or the Scriptures that embody such a fundamental core, Mark. That is what enables the religion of Israel to withstand dissension. Without such a core to fall back on, dissension among believers can be fatal. And such dissension is now rampant. The churches in Palestine view many things differently than the churches in Asia; those in Greece differently than their counterparts in Rome. We have no unifying set of established traditions and writings to set forth our core beliefs, so doctrinal battles even at the fringes threaten to destroy us."

For the first time, I realized that Paul's break with the central writings of Judaism was almost complete. The Jewish Scriptures had become for him a source of prophetic wisdom and historical record rather than a useful guide to salvation. He no longer considered the ultimate tenets of the Torah to form any significant part of the core of his own message. The Law and the Prophets were for him mere historical context, an evolutionary past. Paul had evolved.

What had not changed in Paul, however, was his passionate devotion to his beliefs. The same zeal with which he had tried to expose Christ as a false Messiah thirty years earlier, he later brought to the task of exposing Judaizers as false teachers of the gospel. But now, Paul could no longer tolerate permitting Jewish Christians to worship in accordance with the Law even when they did not seek to persuade Gentile Christians to do likewise—for disparate practices were a threat to unity among the churches, and it was unity that Paul prized above all else. The Body of Christ that all believers comprised may have many different members with many diverse talents and gifts, but when it came to communal worship, Paul insisted that they must all be on the same page. Any Jewish Christian who was perceived to cling to old beliefs was thus a potential foe, including Peter.

Whatever hope I had of persuading Paul that his concerns about Peter were unfounded evaporated with Paul's next question, which took me completely by surprise: "Tell me: have you been commissioned by Peter to commit his memories of the Lord to writing?"

I hesitated only slightly before answering, as I tried to collect myself. "How did you know?"

"I didn't. But Peter surely had some reason for separating you from Timothy in Tarentum, and this one is the most plausible. He is in the twilight of his life, and it is natural for him to want to pass on his memories. He knows that he is no writer, just as he knows that you write well. And for such a task, he would naturally have the greatest trust in someone whom he himself had brought to the faith."

"Then his trust is well-placed. I have assured Peter that I would faithfully record what he related to me."

"And so you shall, Mark, without altering a single word. But as I will not be here to read your account, would you object to sharing his remembrances of the Lord's ministry with me?"

The Cloak and the Parchments   163

Totally disarmed by this request, I found myself unable to voice any reasonable objection to it. The faint suspicion that Paul might somehow seek to manipulate the account despite his assurances to the contrary was quickly replaced by my own curiosity to hear any commentary Paul might have to offer. I would certainly have welcomed his commentary on what was written in the parchments, and I could see no difference between hearing his comments on the parchments and his comments on Peter's stories. In any event, I did not know how long it would be before the opportunity to write would present itself, and I thought that the retelling of Peter's stories might help me to better remember them, perhaps even help me organize them into some semblance of logical order.

And so for the rest of the day, there in Paul's cell, I retold in no particular order Peter's accounts of the miracles, the exorcisms, and the parables and instruction that Jesus had shared with his disciples during his ministry, holding nothing back except for the story of Peter's three denials. Paul listened intently, and did not interrupt me even once. At times I found myself immersed in the tale to the point almost of self-mesmerization. My mental picture of Jesus doing and saying what he did and said was so strong that I almost felt like an eye witness. It was as though I was not relating these things myself, but was merely a mouthpiece of some higher power that took control of my tongue and spoke through me.

In retelling Peter's account of what Jesus had said and done, I began to see for the first time the outline of a recurring theme. Throughout his ministry, Jesus was engaged in a constant struggle with the forces of evil in whatever forms he encountered them, be it demonic possession, sickness, hunger, even the ambition and greed of men—but the more subtle the form of evil, the less direct his efforts to repel it became. He calmed the tempest with a word, and cast out demons the same way. His physical healings typically required an element of faith, whether by the one to be cured or by a friend or relative. But when dealing with sins of pride, lust for power and the like, he resorted to teaching, personal example, and ultimately self-sacrifice. That the power of Satan bent more or less immediately to his will, while the sins of mankind did not, bespoke of the value of free will that Timothy and I had been discussing earlier. No wave of the hand or snap of the fingers would work here; evil lying within in the human heart could be eradicated only through human choice, through a personal decision to heed the will of God. Jesus himself ultimately made such a personal decision, at the greatest of costs to himself. But what I found most fascinating was that just as one person's faith could stand in as the basis for the cure of a loved one, so too could Jesus' bending to the will of God and personal sacrifice serve as a surrogate for others. The message that we were all bound together in this way was becoming clear to me. The war against sin is communal as well as individual, and Jesus expected similar sacrifice from those who would join him in the struggle.

It was late in the day when my narrative ended, after which Paul was quiet and reflective for a full minute at least. "It seems," he observed finally, "that Jesus wished to be secretive about who he was. That secret is now revealed, to those who have the courage and faith to accept it. We will speak more on this another time, Mark. For now, however . . ."

At that moment we heard Timothy and Luke returning, and as they entered the room Paul promptly shifted his focus to Peter. "What news, brothers?"

"Pomponia cannot help us," Luke replied, slightly out of breath. "She and her husband have left the City for their villa in Antium, and are not expected back at least until the fire is controlled. We thought it prudent not to try to see Peter ourselves, but we were able to get a message of encouragement to him through one of the brothers in the Praetorian Guard—at some risk to himself, I might add. And the report is that Peter is fine. He has his own cell, has food and drink, and thus far has been rather well-treated. Tigellinus was preoccupied today with battling the fire, which has apparently now consumed his own house. No doubt he will be in a particularly ugly mood when he returns to deal with Peter."

"Then I must go to see Peter first thing in the morning," I declared. "I am not afraid of arrest, nor will I lead the soldiers back to you if they follow me. Tell me where they are holding him."

"Mark, this is foolishness," Timothy answered me, surprise in his voice. "Peter's captors are just waiting for his friends and benefactors to arrive. Your fate will be the same as his if you go to him."

"What if his guards do not view me as a friend or benefactor? What if they see me not as a visitor but as a slave, come to attend to the prisoners' waste buckets? I can play the part! Perhaps our Praetorian brother can arrange it so that I . . ."

"No," Paul interjected forcefully, "I must forbid this. Your courage is commendable, Mark, but the risk is far too great. There is still much service to the Lord you have yet to give, and you cannot do it from a prison cell. Besides, there is nothing you can do to protect Peter from harm; only God can do that now. Peter will benefit more from your prayers than your presence."

"Then let us pray that God delivers him from his captors again, just as He did years ago when Peter was imprisoned by Herod," I replied.

"I am not familiar with the story," Luke said. "Tell us what happened."

Still in the story-telling mood of the day, I was happy to oblige Luke's request. "When I was a young man in Jerusalem and still living in my mother's house, Peter was arrested. It was soon after Herod had ordered James the brother of John beheaded. Herod saw that James' death was well received by some of the Jews, and he intended the same fate for Peter, but was waiting until the Passover was ended. A number of believers were gathered at our house for the Passover, and we were praying fervently for Peter well into the night.

"There was a knock at the door, and our maid Rhoda went to answer it—but did not open it. Instead, she came back and cried out that it was Peter knocking! 'You are out of your wits!' we said to her, but she insisted she knew his voice and that it was truly him. All this time, the knocking continued. We finally opened the door, and to our astonishment, there he was! He told us that he had been sleeping between two soldiers, fastened with double chains, with two other guards keeping watch at the door, when suddenly an angel of the Lord stood nearby, and light shone in the cell. The angel tapped Peter on the side, woke him and bid him to hurry and get up. With that, the chains dropped from his wrists, and the angel told him to put on his belt, his sandals and his cloak, and follow him. Peter thought it was a mirage, and in a daze followed the angel past both guards, and finally to the iron gate leading into the city, which opened for them of itself. As they made their way down the alley toward our house, the angel left him, and Peter recovered his full senses and realized what had happened. 'Report this to James and the brothers,' Peter told us—and then he left. We were overjoyed, and for the rest of the night we praised God for answering our prayers."

There was a moment of silence in the room. "My brothers," Paul said finally, with an air of reverence, "let us pray."

Chapter 23

The smoke that hung over Rome the next morning told me that the fire was not yet fully quelled, but there were no flames to be seen in the vicinity, and the chaos that had gripped the city seemed to have abated somewhat. Timothy and Luke set out to learn what they could of Peter's inquisition, while I determined to visit Paul and continue our discussion. Deciding that this would be a safe opportunity to bring the parchments to Paul, I gathered them up in his cloak and made my way back to the Praetorian barracks, where the guard befriended by Paul admitted me without so much as a glance to see what I bore in the cloak.

Paul's joy in receiving me became all the greater upon seeing the parchments, as he laid them on top of the collection of scriptures piled beside his bed. "You have done me a great service in bringing them here, Mark, and for this I am grateful. Pray that my failing eyes can endure the strain of passing over these words once again!"

"If you wish it, I will read them to you until my own eyes tire. But I had hoped first to hear your comments on my narrative of yesterday. You did say we would speak further on the subject."

"The very thing I am most anxious to do! We were talking about the Lord's desire that his identity not be publicly revealed, save to those whom he chose. He asked his disciples, 'Who do you say that I am?' Yet when Peter answered that he was the Messiah, he warned them not to disclose that answer to others. The time was not then ripe for his identity to be heralded, for he had not yet come into the glory of the Father. Still today, he poses to all of us the same question, 'Who do you say that I am?' And now that he has risen, we are under no similar restriction in revealing the true answer to others. To the contrary, that is our mission, our sacred charge—and you, Mark, may be privileged to play a special role."

Paul's eyes seemed to pierce right into my soul, as he mouthed the words I knew were coming. "So I ask you, Mark; who do *you* say that Jesus is?"

"He is the Messiah," I answered without trying to sound coy, and waited for the inevitable follow-up question.

"And who is the Messiah? Is it not God Himself, incarnate?"

The doubts that had been gnawing at me for years were all surfacing at once as I considered how to answer. While cast in the guise of a rhetorical question, Paul's inquiry was meant to test me; I knew it, and he knew I did. Even slight hesitation in affirming his premise would disclose that I was unsure, and I had already hesitated slightly. Although I had long known that this moment would arrive, I had no rehearsed response prepared. I decided to deflect the question.

"Peter is not of that view. He sees no declaration in the scriptures that the Messiah would be divine. His view of the Lord is as an *adoptive* son, at best."

"Then perhaps he should read more closely. The Psalms speak of the Messiah as a *begotten* son, not an adopted one—which can only mean that the Messiah must also truly be God."

"But the Psalm says '*This day* I have begotten you.' What of the *previous* day? If indeed this verse refers to the Messiah rather than to David, and 'begotten' is to be understood literally rather than metaphorically, would 'This day' not tend to refute any argument for the Messiah's eternal preexistence?"

"The Psalms also tell us 'For a thousand years in your sight are as yesterday, now that it is past, or as a watch in the night.' Who can say whether the very *first* day was the one referred to? That would mean he existed from the very beginning of time, eternally begotten. Thus does the Book of Genesis refer to God in the plural: 'Let *us* make man in *our* image, after *our* likeness.' 'The man has become like one of *us*, knowing what is good and what is bad.' 'Let *us* then go down and there confuse their language, so that one will not understand what another says.' No, Mark; the Son is as fully God as the Father, and every bit as eternal."

"But if they are *both* God, how can this be squared with the *Shema*? How can the Lord God be One and still speak this way? After all, we are not polytheists. That, more than anything, is the basis of Peter's objection."

"Peter's objection is easily met. The Father and Son are not two Gods, but One—a single divine substance in different manifestations or forms. Form may change, but substance does not. And though Peter once knew the Son in the form of flesh, it is as a living spirit that we know him now—the same living spirit that existed eternally, before his incarnation in the flesh. Thus does Zechariah write:

> 'Sing and rejoice, O daughter Zion! For lo, I am coming to dwell among you, says the Lord. Many nations shall join themselves to the Lord on that day, and they shall be my people; and I will dwell in your midst. And you shall know that the Lord of hosts has sent me to you.'

Here we see the prophesy of the Lord dwelling in our midst, yet being sent by the Lord to do so. Both the one who sends and the one who is sent to dwell with us in the flesh are called 'Lord'—the same Lord in two manifestations.

"Peter is blind to this understanding because he is concerned to integrate Jesus into the fabric of Judaism. But Jesus himself said that this could not be done. I will show you this in the very parchments you brought today." Paul began to peruse them, and then found what he was looking for. "Here it is:

> 'No one sews a piece of unshrunken cloth onto an old cloak; otherwise, the patch pulls away from it, the new from the old, and a worse tear results. And no one puts new wine into old wineskins; otherwise, the wine will burst the skins, and the wine is lost as well as the skins; but one puts new wine into fresh wineskins.'

Jesus was referring to himself as the new patch, and the Torah as the old cloak. He was referring to himself as the new wine, and to the traditional religion of Israel as the old wineskin. If you try to combine the two in a way that forces compatibility, you will fail. Peter does not understand this. The fresh wineskin that can hold the concept of Jesus' true identity is foreign to Peter, who is inflexibly enmeshed in the old way of thinking."

Tempted though I was to challenge Paul's interpretation, I knew that both his powers of argument and his command of Scripture were vastly superior to mine, and inevitably I would lose the debate. I opted instead to continue the discussion in the relative safety of pressing Peter's views, rather than my own doubts.

"Yet Peter relates that in all their time together he overheard not a single claim by Jesus to be divine—not publicly, not to the disciples privately, not even to the Sanhedrin that reputedly sought his execution due to his blasphemy in claiming to be the Son of God."

"It is more than repute which confirms his having made such a claim before the Sanhedrin, Mark; it is simple logic. Of what other capital offense aside from blasphemy could Jesus possibly have been convicted?"

"But Peter points out that under Jewish law the penalty for blasphemy is stoning, not crucifixion."

"You presume, incorrectly, that despite being under Roman rule the Sanhedrin retained the authority to put a man to death in accordance with Jewish law."

"I presume only that any Roman restrictions on Jewish executions would not deter a zealous mob from implementing the command of the Torah. Were you yourself not present when they stoned Stephen to death?"

Paul's angry scowl betrayed the offense he took at this remark, and I instantly regretted the comment. Not only had I abandoned whatever safety might lie in casting my objections as Peter's own, but I had crossed an emotional line by making reference to Paul's former life as a persecutor of the early followers of Christ. Paul's response took on the same tone with which he had sparred with Peter upon our arrival.

"The Sanhedrin was no mob of zealots impassioned into religious frenzy by a surprise declaration. They had planned this indictment carefully to bait him into this admission, going so far as to meet at night during the Passover in violation of the Torah. Clearly the commands of the Torah were not foremost on their minds; they had too much to lose by flaunting Roman law in their retribution, and much to gain by pointing to Pilate rather than themselves as executioner."

"I see your point."

"And do you also see that they must have anticipated that he would claim to be the Son of God during their interrogation—which makes sense only if he had publicly so claimed before?"

"That is a fair inference, I agree, but one which makes Peter's testimony—or the lack of it—all the more stark. If Jesus did indeed make such a claim, would we not expect *some* remembrance of it by Peter? Are you not troubled that Peter never overheard such a claim even once?"

"Never *overheard*, Mark; or never *understood*? Peter attests that Jesus spoke in parables which even his disciples sometimes had difficulty understanding—and that can only mean that he was concerned to veil the full truth even from them. You related yesterday the parable of the faithless tenants, who beat or killed all those sent by the vineyard owner to collect a share of the produce, including ultimately the owner's own son, and then incurred the owner's wrath. It is obvious that the scribes who heard this parable took Jesus' words as a reference to his own divine sonship, for they immediately plotted to do away with him as a blasphemer—even if Peter and the disciples did not so understand the reference.

"Likewise when the scribes accused him of casting out demons by the power of Satan, and Jesus declared that all sins would be forgiven except for blasphemy against the Holy Spirit; he was not contrasting blasphemy against God with blasphemy against himself, but rather condemning the scribes for claiming that his own miracles were not the work of God. That was nothing less than asserting the power of God as his own, regardless of how his disciples took it."

"Suppose you are right, and Peter and the Twelve simply missed the message," I replied, although I found it remarkable that such a key truth would be kept hidden from the very inner circle that Jesus had called to himself to spread his message. "Even so, surely we would expect *some* declaration during his time here on earth, by *some*one, that Jesus was indeed the Son of God."

"Why do you presume that there was none? Yesterday you related Peter's account of the exorcism in the synagogue in Capernaum, of the demon shrieking at Jesus and calling him the Holy One of God. The true meaning of that appellation may have been hidden from those present because they were not yet ready to receive such a transcendent truth, but the demon surely recognized Jesus for who he was—not simply as an emissary or prophet, but as the Son of God. I dare say there must have been similar recognitions from other expelled demons as well, whether or not Peter heard them or understood their language."

Despite the urge to protest that a variant of the appellation "Holy One of God" had been used in scripture to describe Aaron, Elijah, Elisha and others, I made no challenge to Paul's interpretation of how the demon in the synagogue had intended the phrase. But the presumption that other exorcisms had elicited like recognitions from other demonic spirits gave me pause. "Even if that is so, Paul, it was not *Peter's* account, and I have promised to commit *his* account to writing, faithfully in every respect."

"It is consistent with Peter's account, and anything you write which is consistent with his account does not break your promise to him. His is not the only possible witness to Jesus' true nature. Tell me, would you be more at ease with the lack of Peter's testimony if you had the testimony of scripture?"

Before I could answer, Paul reached for one of the scrolls next to his bed and spread it in front of us. "In the Wisdom of Solomon, it is written:

> Let us lie in wait for the righteous man, because he is inconvenient to us and opposes our actions; he reproaches us for sins against the law, and accuses us of violating our training. He professes to have knowledge of God, and calls himself a child of the Lord. He has become to us a reproof of our thoughts; the very sight of him is a burden to us, because his manner of life is not like that of others, and his ways are strange. We are considered by him as something base, and he avoids our paths as though we were unclean; he calls the destiny of the just blessed, and boasts that God is his father. Let us see if his words be true, and let us test what will happen at the end of his life; for if the just one is the son of God, he will help him, and will deliver him from the hand of his foes. Let us test him with insult and torture, that we may have proof of his gentleness, and try his forbearance. Let us condemn him to a shameful death, for, according to what he says, he will be protected.

The Cloak and the Parchments

Who will deny that this passage speaks precisely the point of view of the Jews who condemned Jesus to death?"

Although the Book of Wisdom was a comparatively recent work and not of the same stature as more ancient and traditional texts, I had to admit that it would not be unreasonable to read the passage as presaging Jesus' death. Still, I was not convinced that its reference to the son of God should be taken in as literal a sense as Paul obviously meant it.

"But has not the phrase 'son of God' been applied to Solomon and other ancient kings of Judah descendant from David, as an honorific title? How are we to understand the term as used in this passage any differently?"

"This passage does not speak of a king, Mark. Surely that much is clear to you!"

"True; but this passage speaks of one who claimed that God would protect him from harm—yet according to Peter, Jesus several times claimed the opposite, that suffering and death rather than deliverance would be his fate."

"Oh? Can there be any greater deliverance than resurrection?"

I was not persuaded. "Is this, then, the scripture that convinces you of the divinity of Christ?"

"I need no scripture to convince *me*! The gospel I preach came by revelation from Jesus Christ himself. *He* revealed himself to me as the true Son of God."

Paul's claim of direct revelation, the same claim he had made in his letter to the Galatians and at various times to me and other followers, was an instant debate ender. One could dispute his interpretation of ancient texts, or challenge the inferences he drew from other facts or events—such as the declaration in the first sentence of his letter to the Romans that Jesus' resurrection itself proclaims him to be the Son of God—but there can be no argument, by appeal to scripture or anything else, once the claim of direct revelation has been made. The issue is immediately shifted from one of logic and verification to one of trust and faith—precisely the struggle that had plagued me for years.

Paul understood this well, as his voice grew gentler and his steady eyes held me in their gaze. "You have a higher calling than that of a mere recorder of one man's reminiscences, Mark. You have an opportunity to mold those memories into a story that will bring to life the true glorious message of the gospel—that God has manifested Himself to mankind by assuming a human nature in indissoluble union with Himself, and that Jesus of Nazareth is that incarnate Son of God, belief in whose atoning death and resurrection leads to the forgiveness of sins and salvation for Jews and Gentiles alike. It is in this context that any eyewitness account of our Lord's earthly ministry must be presented. No writer could undertake a more important task. The question is, Mark, are you prepared to undertake it?"

Chapter 24

The following morning I was awakened by the hand of Timothy grabbing my shoulder. "Quickly, Mark, get up! There is trouble."

"What is it?" I asked, half-awake and rubbing the sleep from my eyes.

"It is Peter," Timothy replied. "He is being taken before Nero this morning, accused of masterminding the fire!"

I sprang to my feet in an instant, and saw that Luke and Rufus were in the room as well. "Tell me what you know," I demanded.

"Luke and I have been up most of the night trying to learn more of the details. We saw Peter late in the day yesterday as he was being removed from his cell and led away in chains toward Tigellinus' headquarters. Throughout the evening, our sources in the Guard have kept us as informed as they could without revealing themselves, or us, to the Prefect's henchmen. Now, at Tigellinus' suggestion, it appears that Peter is to be arraigned directly before Nero, who wishes to question Peter personally about his role in the fire. We know the place, but not the time, so we need to hurry if we are to be certain of seeing him."

"Is there any chance for escape?" I asked, hoping against hope, and knowing that if Peter were convicted before Nero it would be certain death for him.

"None," Luke answered. "The brothers in the Guard are powerless to stop this. But they say they may be able to admit one or two of us into the outer courtyard, not close enough to hear the proceedings but with a clear view of Peter when they take him back to his cell. Timothy and I have already agreed that it should be you and he who try to gain entrance. Rufus and I will assemble as many of the elders as we can and wait here for you."

I was dressed and ready to leave by the time Luke had finished speaking. Timothy and I rushed out of the house without a thought to food, drink or even prayer, and hurried on our way, skirting as best we could the sections of the City which were still smoldering. As we walked through the narrow and smoky streets, I recalled Peter's silent realization during our journey to Rome that his final days were at hand. I made no mention of this to Timothy. I desperately wanted to believe that somehow God would arrange a way for Peter to escape, as he had many years ago in Jerusalem. But I knew also that Peter would resist any effort to deliver him from his fate, for fear of retribution against the entire community of believers. The most we could hope for was that our presence might somehow offer him a measure of encouragement.

Before long we arrived at the courtyard gate, where one of the soldiers with whom Timothy and Luke had arranged a signal the night before stood among the guards, and shot us a look of recognition. Timothy approached, and with the edge of his sandal traced a crude fish in the dirt before him, thus letting the soldier know that we were here to see the fisherman from Galilee. Immediately he ordered the gate opened, and we were inside.

Aside from a few soldiers who stood at the fountain in the center of the courtyard, congratulating themselves on their good fortune in having escaped firefighting duties that day, the place was filled with the comings and goings of slaves and patricians, each on an apparent mission, none of them loitering. Realizing that we would be conspicuous by our inactivity, Timothy and I found our way to a spot behind the gardens in a far corner more or less out of the soldiers' view, and did our best to blend into the vines that crept up the walls of the yard. Fortunately they were oblivious to us, for if they demanded to know our business we would surely have a difficult time justifying our presence. Was this how Peter had felt as he waited in the courtyard of the Sanhedrin the night that Jesus was arrested—the night of his threefold denial? How ironic that I should be in a similar position years later, awaiting the result of Peter's own arraignment!

What little we could hear in the discussions of the passers-by seemed all to be on a common theme: the cause of the fire. More than one muttered that they would not be surprised if Nero himself had ordered the blaze, perhaps to clear a space for the building of a new palace, or simply out of sheer madness. The unpredictable and ill-tempered Emperor had lost his initial popularity, and was now feared by many in the City, whether slave, freedman or upper-class noble. The grain he furnished for free to a large segment of the populace, and the games he commissioned to entertain the masses, secured him but little affection. Such gestures had proven insufficient to overcome the silent derision and even contempt fostered by his base pretensions to art, to singing and to acting. Even those within his patronage, who tolerated his whims purely for personal advantage, now viewed him as half-insane and an almost comic figure, egotistical and mean-spirited. And Tigellinus, whose transparent ambitions were matched only by his cruelty, had the Emperor's ear. Such was the ruler in whose hands Peter's fate resided. There was nothing I could do for the great disciple of Christ—except to keep my promise to him.

"Peter has asked me to write his memoirs of Jesus," I confided to Timothy. "Our trip up from Tarentum was occupied by little else than his recollections. And write them I shall."

"How appropriate," Timothy responded. "He said that his purpose in coming was to strengthen the Roman church, and now you will have an opportunity to be the vehicle for his doing precisely that. His mission will be fulfilled, no matter how this day turns out." We both knew that it would almost certainly turn out badly, but neither of us wished to mention the obvious.

"Yet I am conflicted, Timothy; I am not sure what to write. Oh, Peter's memories are clear enough, and the sayings recorded in the parchments will be useful source material as well, but weaving it all into a story that carries the proper message—that will be problematic, I fear."

"What is your concern?"

"It's just that Peter's account lacks the theological message Paul feels I should be including. Paul is completely focused on the principle that the new life of the believer is centered on the risen and exalted Christ. For Paul, it was not the Lord's preaching or miracles that ushered in the kingdom of God, but his redeeming acts, his death, resurrection and exaltation to a ruling position in heaven; his risen life alone defines and sustains his church. As Paul sees it, any view of the kingdom based solely on the bare record of Christ's earthly life must inevitably miss this point, a point that he insists must be stressed in any theologically valid account of that earthly life. But it is a message that, in significant respects, Peter does not agree with."

"Are you referring to their disagreements over the continued validity of Jewish law?"

"It goes deeper than that, Timothy; much deeper. Paul's teaching that Jesus is the literal Son of God is disputed by Peter. He sees neither evidence for such a conclusion nor need for it, and questions its consistency with the fundamental tenets of Judaism. Paul, on the other hand, is adamant on the truth of this basic proposition."

"I see. And how do you plan to resolve this dilemma?"

"I have no idea! Pray for guidance, I suppose."

"So you should. And I will pray with you. God, and ultimately your heart, must guide you. You already know that I am inclined to Paul's view on this, so I think it would not be proper for me to try to influence your decision by pressing for Paul's position."

"Timothy, do not feel that way! I would be happy to hear argument both for and against Paul's view, from those whose opinions I respect—and you know that I respect your opinions. I need all the help I can get!"

"If it is argument you wish to hear, in truth I am not sure that I or anyone else can offer you much help. Once again you are seeking a rational, logical basis for a decision that in the end can only be guided by faith. Your quest to square the Way with Greek philosophy is getting in the way.

"Trust your own feelings, Mark. What I urged you to do at the beginning of our journey, I urge you to do now: use those feelings as your guide for what is true. If an answer *feels* right in the depths of your soul, you must let that feeling guide you even if logical evidence or rational demonstration may be lacking. For logic can never supplant faith in such a case."

Timothy was right, of course. No personal struggle of faith could be resolved by reasoned arguments or empirical evidence. But recognizing that fact brought me no closer to a resolution.

"My problem, Timothy, is that in this instance *both* perspectives feel right in the depths of my soul! I want to trust that God will guide me, but how can I recognize God's guidance in such a case? What guide can I use *then*? There must be a way to keep my vow to Peter, recording his stories accurately while still letting the spirit lead me to add the proper context to his remembrances. But I am not being led, in *any* direction! It is as if I have erected some barricade around my soul to keep such inspiration out, a barricade I cannot even recognize, much less tear down."

"I see. You believe that God has endowed us with the freedom to resist His entrance into our souls, to put up obstacles which block that entrance."

"I do."

"And what obstacles are those?"

"Pride, envy, greed, lust, intolerance, anger, malice . . . there are many such obstacles. But I cannot identify the one at work here."

"With all due respect, Mark, you give yourself too much credit. If God made our souls in His own image, He can easily find His way into them. We cannot keep Him out. Just remain open to being led, and eventually you will be."

I hoped that Timothy was right. Perhaps it was only trust and patience that I lacked. And I offered a silent prayer that God would grant me both.

At last, after waiting for most of the morning, we spotted Peter, being led into the courtyard from within the walls of the atrium by four guards, hands tied behind his back, a rope around his neck. As we moved out into the open, toward the gate where he would be sure to see us, my heart pounded in my chest, and my throat tightened to the point that I could not swallow.

When our eyes met, Peter's gaunt face seemed to shine, and he managed a faint smile before looking away. As he passed by us, he gazed straight ahead so as not to give us away, and said in Aramaic,

"Be at peace. I go to meet the Lord." And with that brief word to sustain our spirits, he was led through the gate and out into the street.

The sadness of the moment quickly overshadowed Peter's inspirational courage. Here we had come to give encouragement to him, and true to form, his sole concern was to offer the same to us, letting us know that he had no fear of death, and perhaps even welcomed it. But my faith was failing me, and I could take little encouragement from his words. My mind raced with possibilities, none of them welcome. Would they execute him right away? Would they torture him first in an effort to have him confess to some conspiracy? A wave of dizziness overcame me suddenly, and I felt that I would have swooned if Timothy had not taken my arm to support me. "Easy, Mark. Breathe deeply, and collect yourself. Can you walk? Come, let us go; there is nothing more for us here."

I managed to recover my composure, and as we left the courtyard Timothy suggested that I report to Paul what we had seen, while he returned to Rufus' house to do the same. We agreed to meet at Paul's cell before sunset, and went our separate ways, he toward the Campus Martius, I toward the Praetorian barracks.

I was not to see Timothy again for many years.

Chapter 25

Pacing around his cell, Paul showed grave concern as I related the events of the morning and the evident result of Peter's hearing before Nero. "As tragic as it is, this sentence was hardly unexpected," he observed when I was finished. "I could see that Tigellinus was bent on Peter's destruction from the look in his eyes when they met here in this cell. What is surprising, though, is that Tigellinus saw the need to bring Peter before Nero at all. He could have had Peter executed on his own authority without even the pretense of a trial, as Peter is not a Roman citizen. Peter would be accorded no greater rights than a slave."

"'No man's a slave who does not fear to die,'" I quoted Euripides.

"Peter is a slave to the Lord, as are we all. And now, we are all equally at risk. That the Emperor's time was taken up with this matter indicates only one thing to me: Tigellinus is indeed seeking to blame the fire on Christians, and is asking Nero to issue an edict for their punishment. May God give all of us courage and strength!"

I felt my stomach knotting again as I resisted the notion that a persecution of the believers in Rome might ensue. "How can you be sure, Paul? And even if you are right, how do we know the Emperor will issue that edict?"

"As long as Tigellinus basks in imperial favor, Nero will indulge his whims and suspicions, particularly regarding what the emperor regards as a dangerous cult. Moreover, the speculation you overheard in the courtyard today about Nero himself ordering the blaze may well reflect popular opinion. If a scapegoat is needed to deflect suspicion from the emperor, one has now been found. At the very least, the leaders among the brethren will be rounded up, and I fear there may be a rash of imprisonments and executions."

There was no need for Paul to mention the fact that he himself would surely be the most obvious target of that retribution. Yet watching his face, I could see no trace of fear, only concern for the church he loved. Paul faced his fate with the same serenity that Peter had. As devastated as I was by the thought of losing both of them to the executioner at the same time, I could not help but feel buttressed by their faith.

"How soon do you think this will happen?" I asked.

"Very soon indeed. And that is why it would be best for you to leave the City at once."

Suddenly I thought back to my split-up with Paul years earlier in Pamphylia. Was Paul expecting me to run away again? Whether he was or not, I was determined to show him that I was not a coward. His courage, as well as Peter's calm bravery in the courtyard, gave me all the inspiration I needed. "No, Paul," I protested with all the bravado I could muster. "I'm not going anywhere. Did not the Lord say *'Whoever would save his life will lose it, but whoever loses his life for my sake and the gospel's will save it'*? Even if it means I must die with you and with Peter, this time I am not abandoning my post! You called me here from Ephesus, and here I will stay. I am not afraid. I will stay by your side no matter what persecutions may come, and remain faithful until the end."

As soon as I uttered these words, I recalled Peter's similar pronouncement to Jesus on the night of his arrest, and Peter's subsequent triple denial. The courage that I had felt a moment earlier dissipated as quickly as it had come on. But Paul did not seem to notice.

"Your leaving Rome *is* for the sake of the gospel. You have important writing to do. *That* is your calling; *that* is your ministry now. And that is what I ask of you, Mark. Whatever tribulations befall those of us who must stay behind are but the culmination of the Lord's will for us—but not for you. You can give no greater service than to instruct and encourage those who will remain to face persecution for his sake. And that service is now urgent. The example of the Lord, who embraced and endured suffering for the sake of humanity, will serve to strengthen the resolve of the faithful when they too must suffer for his sake."

Paul took the parchments and spread them out on his cot. "These are the times of persecution that the Lord foretold. Here in these parchments it is written:

> *When men bring you to trial and hand you over, do not worry beforehand about what you are to say, but say whatever you are inspired to say, for it is not you who will speak but the Holy Spirit. Brother will hand over brother for execution, and a father his child, and children will turn against their parents and have them put to death. You will be hated by all because of my name. But the one who endures to the end will be saved.*

This is the message that must now be brought to the church at Rome, and you are the chosen instrument for doing so. Do not resist this calling, Mark. You have the talent, the tools, and, I pray to God, the desire to spread the message of love and salvation for which many will give their earthly lives and enter into the kingdom of heaven."

Whether it was my quickly failing courage or the prospect of offering a greater service through my writing that propelled my answer, I did not protest further. "Very well," I agreed. "I will go."

"Good. There is little time to lose, so do not tarry. Do not even return to Rufus' house for your belongings; God will provide whatever you need. Beyond the Aventine Hill you will reach the wharves at the Emporium, where you can board a barge and travel down the Tiber to Ostia. From there, you can follow the coast road to Antium, where you must find Pomponia Graecina's villa. I will write a letter of introduction for you; she will protect you, and if necessary arrange your safe transit out of Italy."

"What about Timothy? He is to meet us here by sunset; should we not travel to Antium together?"

"No. I have use for Timothy here. Besides, you must depart at once if you are to catch a barge before they have all put in for the evening."

As Paul hurriedly retrieved a piece of papyrus and began writing, I was suddenly overwhelmed by a sense of responsibility—and once again of self-doubt. The two men I admired most in the world were both facing death for the cause of Christ, and each of them had solemnly commissioned me on a task of the greatest importance. What would be my legacy to them? How would I manage to harmonize their divergent views—and if I could not, which one would I fail? Could I end up failing both of them?

There will be time to indulge such doubts after getting safely out of Rome, I thought to myself as Paul pressed the letter into my hand. "Give this to Pomponia, and she will be pleased to furnish you with whatever you require. You must take the parchments with you as well. Obviously they are no longer safe here with me, and they will be of much use to you."

At that moment, I could find no words to speak what was in my heart. Tears welled in my eyes as I realized that I would never see Paul again, at least not in this world. Paul's eyes, however, remained dry and calm, almost comforting. The steadfast champion of the Faith, the beacon to the Gentiles that I so admired, handed me the parchments and smiled reassuringly. "May the full truth that lies within these scrolls be made clear to you, Mark. I have no doubt that you will find the inspiration you seek. Kneel for my blessing." I went down on my knees and bowed as Paul placed his hands on my head and prayed aloud that the Lord would ensure my safety and guide my mission.

We embraced for the last time, and I turned to go. "Wait!" Paul called to me as I knocked at the door for the guard to let me out. He reached down next to his cot, picked up his cloak and presented it to me. "For the winter," he said simply, recognizing that I would be the only one of us who would live to see that season again.

Or was his passing this mantle meant to impress upon me that he now considered me, in some small way, as a successor to his ministry?

Chapter 26

Although the meandering Tiber was navigable to smaller craft between Rome and the sea, larger merchant vessels were obliged to discharge their cargos at the mouth of the river in Ostia, where hundreds of barges were employed to ferry their contents up to the Imperial City. As often as not these barges returned downriver relatively empty, which made it all the easier for me to find one willing to take me along. I would be in Ostia by nightfall.

Per Paul's suggestion, I did not stop to retrieve anything from Rufus' house. My only possessions were the tunic on my back, the sandals on my feet, and the letter, cloak and parchments that Paul had given me. The tillerman was kind enough to share a bit of bread and fruit with me, for which I thanked him warmly. I settled in the stern next to him to collect my thoughts as we made our way down the Tiber, and for the first time since my arrival in Rome the acrid smell of smoldering wood, soot and ash no longer hung in the air, replaced by the foul odor of the river itself.

As the river widened and the tillerman guided the barge to the center of the stream, it demanded less than his complete attention, much of which he then turned to me. "Have you family or friends in Ostia?" he inquired. But despite his kindness toward me, I was tired, and not in the mood to make conversation.

"Neither one," I replied.

"Meeting a ship, perhaps?"

"No."

He glanced at the cloak and parchments. "You travel quite light, then."

I made no answer, but the tillerman persisted. "Still, it is good that you thought to bring a cloak. We will be getting some rain tonight, finally. There is little shelter to be found in the harbor, and you will want to keep that precious scroll dry as well as yourself."

"What do you know of its worth?" I demanded. "And how do you know I will not be staying at an inn?"

He pushed at the rudder and grinned into the gathering clouds ahead. "You are a foreigner, and have neither food, nor money to buy any. You had to leave Rome in a hurry, with enough time only to take what you truly needed, and you chose those parchments. Moreover," he added, "your soul is troubled, as though by some momentous choice you must make but cannot decide upon."

"You are most observant, sir. But only God can look into a man's soul."

"And were God to look into yours, what trouble would He see?"

"None you can help me with, I am afraid—unless you have a way to transport me to Antium tonight."

"That I do not. Antium is nearly a day's walk from Ostia, and I would not advise attempting it in darkness and rain. But tomorrow morning I can get you on a boat heading down the coast. There are several that make the trip between the two ports each day, and I am friendly with their captains. If you wish, you can take shelter from the rain tonight at my house, and when you awake I will take you to them. Then, perhaps, your troubles will ease a bit."

The tillerman's generosity to a complete stranger was as unexpected as it was welcome. "Your assistance is greatly appreciated, sir. I cannot pay you, for it is as you say, I have no money. Nor is it likely that I will pass this way again."

"No matter. I will consider it payment in full if you offer similar aid to a stranger when next you find yourself in a position to do so."

Intrigued by the remarkable charity this man displayed, I was curious to find out what I could of his beliefs. "I see that you are a man of true virtue, sir. Is it in the service of God that you extend such charity to your fellow man?"

"Not in the sense that you mean it, my friend, although I believe that the gods are virtuous and wish for humanity to be so as well. But I follow no particular religious doctrine or practices. Rather, I am an adherent to the teachings of that most excellent philosopher Musonius Rufus, who lectures in Rome. Perhaps you have heard of him?"

"I confess that I have not. What is his philosophy?"

"Musonius teaches that we all have by nature a capacity for virtue, an ability to overcome and resist the corruption, selfishness and evil we find all about us, but that this can only be done by diligently developing the several qualities of virtue—prudence, temperance, courage and justice—for it is these which lead to perfection of the soul, and thence to true happiness. Once these qualities of virtue are fully developed and practiced—which is the very aim of philosophy—all vices and evils can be overcome and the good life can be achieved, as one recognizes that it is worse to do a wrong than to suffer one, better to do good than to receive it at the hands of another."

As the tillerman related this, I was struck by the parallels between Musonius' beliefs and the exhortations to charity and love that Paul preached. Was the overlap coincidental? I needed to find out. "Much of what you say describes the beliefs of Christians such as myself. We are likewise instructed that love of our neighbor must be a guiding principle of our lives, second only to love of God. Tell me; are you familiar with the teachings of Paul of Tarsus?"

"To some extent; not with his religious teachings, but with his ethics. Some time ago, Musonius read to us from a letter he had acquired, written by this man Paul and addressed to the Roman followers of your Christ. I recall that his letter urged them to let their love be genuine; to hate what is evil, and cling to what is good; to love one another with brotherly affection and to outdo one another in showing respect. He charged them to contribute to the needs of other believers, to practice hospitality and live in harmony with one another, rejoicing with those who rejoice, weeping with those who weep. He taught that they should not be haughty, but associate with the lowly without conceit, acting honorably in the eyes of all, and if possible living peaceably with all. He counseled them to bless rather than curse those who persecute them, to repay no evil with evil, nor seek to avenge themselves, but to leave vengeance to God. He wrote, 'If your enemy is hungry, feed him; if he is thirsty, give him drink; and do not be overcome by evil, but overcome evil with good.' With all of these teachings, the followers of Musonius are in general agreement."

"It seems, then, that you and I are of like understanding of the virtuous life. But we who follow the path of Christ believe that the true purpose of such a life is to bring us into a right relation with the one true God of Israel, the Creator of the universe, whose grace has been poured out for humanity through His anointed one, Jesus of Nazareth, and who offers eternal life to those who believe in him and follow the example of compassion and love that he set for us."

"Perhaps we will differ somewhat here. I do not look to eternal life as a reward for being virtuous. To quote from Ovid, 'virtue is its own reward.' If the gods wish to add a further prize, they are free to do so, but to look to that prize as the motive for our actions would render our motives less than pure. The pursuit of virtue for what it may bring us in terms of an eternal reward rather than for its own sake threatens to make our actions basically selfish—and that is in some respects the antithesis of virtue."

The tillerman's words brought back those of Peter during our trip up the Italian peninsula, recounting Jesus' caution to the Twelve not to adopt the attitude of those who sacrifice because of the hope of future reward. Here before me was a man who had adopted precisely the attitude Jesus expounded, and I marveled at his insight.

"But do you even believe in the afterlife of the human soul?" I asked him.

"I believe it is possible."

"And what of bodily resurrection, and eternal life in the flesh?"

"Ah, that is quite different! I do not see how that is possible. In any event, it is idle to speculate on the possibility, as there can be no evidence of such life after death—unless someone were to come back from the dead and attest to it."

"Indeed," I replied. "And since we believe that Jesus of Nazareth has done precisely that, we cling to that hope for ourselves as well. For it is attested that he was crucified, and afterwards he rose from the dead and appeared to hundreds before finally ascending bodily into heaven. Some of those who saw him after his resurrection are still alive."

"Were you one of those to whom he appeared?"

"No."

"So then, you are relying on the testimony of other witnesses whose veracity you accept."

"Yes."

"But you yourself cannot testify as an eyewitness."

"No."

"How then can you hope to persuade others? Indeed, once the last eyewitness has passed on, how can *any* more be persuaded?"

"In the same manner that thousands have come to believe in the resurrection despite never having heard the testimony of an eyewitness. Some are persuaded of the truth of the resurrection through the example shown by adherents to the faith, who demonstrate that Jesus truly lives on in them through the reformation of their own lives, practicing the love and charity that Jesus admonished his followers to practice."

"But you yourself observed a few minutes ago that the disciples of Musonius, who are not Christians, demonstrate the same love of others that Christians adopt as a guiding principle of their own lives. How can the truth of any Christian doctrine, whether it be the resurrection of this Jesus or some other tenet, be inferred from the path of virtue that believers follow, when such virtue is not an exclusive trait of Christians?"

"I do not mean to suggest that the virtuous lives of believers are the sole evidence that Jesus lives. Others have come to be persuaded through miraculous cures by and of those who have faith in his continued power. Why, in Tarentum only a few weeks ago, a hunchback was baptized in the name of Jesus, and immediately his spine was straightened, in front of dozens of witnesses, myself included. Many of those witnesses and their families came to believe in the power of God that resides in the name of Jesus that very day."

"And what of those who have witnessed no miracles personally? Are they likewise to be persuaded by the testimony of eyewitnesses whose veracity they accept?"

"Yes."

"It would seem, then, that the continued spread of your religion must be dependant on a more or less steady stream of such miracles —for otherwise, as eyewitnesses begin to disappear, so will the testimony required to persuade new believers."

"Not at all—unless we allow that miracles need not entail adjusting the laws of nature, and can occur solely in the heart. A conviction of certainty may come through direct experience of the divine, as God Himself reveals His truth to those who seek Him. For those who come to believe through such revelation, the experience cannot be adequately described in words, but its reality is undeniable to them. They are not *eye*-witnesses, since what they perceive is through the heart rather than the eyes—but they are witnesses nonetheless. And there are some to whom God has revealed that Jesus not only lives in the flesh, but that it was impossible for death to hold him because he is indeed God Himself, made incarnate in the person of Jesus."

As I spoke, I thought back to the reaction I had had to Paul's claim of direct revelation of the divinity of Jesus. There was no way either to verify or disprove such a claim, and I half-expected the tillerman to challenge it on that basis. But he surprised me again.

"Yes," he said, "you are right; I was mistaken. I can foresee a religion gaining adherents in such a way. If believers agree among themselves that such a direct revelation has indeed been shared by them and yields in each of them the same certainty of the same thing, then I suppose it must be accepted by others as true even without further proof."

"And why do you say so?" I asked.

"When others perceive something that we ourselves have not perceived—let us say a rainbow over Ostia, or earthquake tremors in Pompeii—even though we may be unable to verify it independently of their testimony, we nevertheless assume that what they say they perceived has a basis in reality, at least in the absence of some evidence that they have been deluded or possess some motive to falsify their account. And if we make this assumption with respect to something perceived by others with their five senses, I see no reason to make a different assumption simply because their common perception is the result of a religious experience. Unless I am to deny the possibility of religious experience altogether—which I am not prepared to do

—then to be consistent, I must credit such shared perceptions in whatever form they occur."

"That is a most enlightened view, sir. I pray that God further enlightens you by revealing His truth to you as well, and also rewards you for your kindness, whether you seek such a reward or not."

The tillerman acknowledged my good wishes with a gracious nod and a broad smile, gazing ahead into the dusk as we neared the wharfs of Ostia. And as he guided the barge into position to dock, a faint roll of thunder broke the still evening air, and the first drops of rain I had felt since leaving Ephesus began to fall.

Chapter 27

The following morning, thanks to the tillerman's connections, I secured a berth on board a small cargo boat bound for Antium, and by early afternoon I found myself sailing past its opulent hillside and beachside villas, summer retreats of the Roman aristocracy. At my request the captain pointed out the villa of Aulus Plautius, an impressive ivy-covered structure set back from the water.

Once we had tied up in port I wasted no time making my way up the beach toward the villa. On reaching the gates, I announced myself to a gardener as bearing an urgent letter for Pomponia. He promptly fetched the *maior domus*, to whom I handed my letter of introduction, whereupon I was escorted by two slaves into the courtyard to await her arrival. I did not have long to wait.

Pomponia's face, although showing signs of her advanced age, had a gentle serenity that immediately comforted the beholder. She took both my hands in hers and gave them a tiny squeeze as she welcomed me. "Paul's letter says that you are a writer, and his dear friend and fellow servant of Christ, and as such, know that I am in *your* service. Come, you must be tired. I will have refreshments prepared for us, and you can bathe and relax while my servants find you some new clothes. Please consider this villa your home for as long as you wish to stay."

Within an hour I was resting in the inner garden with the parchments at my side, sharing some bread, wine and goat cheese with Pomponia and relating the events of the past days since Peter and

I had arrived in Rome. The noble lady listened intently without interruption, tears occasionally wetting her eyes. She knew Tigellinus well, and what cruelty he was capable of inflicting.

"I share Paul's concern about persecution of Christians," she told me when I had finished. "Rumors abound that Nero himself ordered Rome to be set ablaze. He was here in Antium when the fire broke out, but in recent weeks he was often overheard decrying the stench and squalor of the City; once he even commented that he wished it would burn to the ground so that he could build it anew. Nero is a vain man, and he will seek to quash such rumors any way he can, even if it is by casting the blame for this fire onto innocents. He will welcome Tigellinus' suggestions on how best to accomplish this, even if it be to quench the embers of this fire with the blood of martyrs."

"All the more reason, my lady, for me to be about my business as soon as possible: to write an account of our Lord's ministry on earth. These parchments I have with me contain many of the Lord's sayings, and I have as well Peter's remembrances of his teachings. If, by God's grace, I am able to strengthen the faith of believers by recounting the example of our Lord in enduring suffering and death, I am anxious to do so. What I need is a safe and quiet place to undertake the task."

"That much I can offer you here. There is a comfortable guest room upstairs overlooking the sea, well lit and perfect for reflection. You will want for nothing; I will have writing materials, your meals, and anything you wish brought to you. I will see to it that you are not disturbed."

"Thank you, my lady. I hope that your hospitality will not be needed longer than you intend to extend it, for you should know that it may take me quite some time to finish. Indeed, at this moment I am not sure how even to begin."

"Then you must pray that God will guide your hand. I will pray as well. You are undertaking a task of great importance, and you must not rush it on my account."

We bowed our heads in a short prayer, and I was shown to the room that was to be my home for the next several weeks. Pomponia's description of the room as being comfortable was an extreme understatement; after the Spartan accommodations I was used to, it was nothing short of luxurious. I sat on the freshly pressed linens of the bed and gazed out of the window at the shimmering Tyrrhenian sea, feeling its soothing breeze on my face—and quickly thought of Paul in his cell, and Peter in his. Why should I be so favored when they were bereft of all comforts, perhaps even in torment? This was no time to bask in the pleasures of my quarters or to enjoy the vista outside my window. I determined to begin working at once.

But how to start? What do I write?

I realized that I needed to make a choice right at the outset between two competing approaches: relating Peter's eyewitness account of Jesus' words and deeds without theological interpretation, or casting them in terms of Paul's theology, particularly his insistence on Jesus' divinity. The guidance I had prayed for in wrestling with this dilemma did not seem to be forthcoming; I was no closer to a resolution than ever, and the visceral feeling that Timothy had suggested I use as my test for what was true was completely absent.

I recalled what Timothy had said at the beginning of our trip about the need for Paul's contrary views to bow to what Peter reported that Jesus himself has said. But Timothy's observation was no help to me here; Paul was surely right that anything I wrote which was consistent with Peter's account could not render my story unfaithful to it. I was faced with the converse issue. Inconsistency with eyewitness testimony might call a proposition into question, but consistency with it certainly did not render the proposition true.

Peter himself had been careful to note that he was not claiming Paul's views on Jesus' divinity to be false—only that they were lacking in evidence, unnecessary to the saving efficacy of Jesus' sacrifice, and difficult to reconcile with some things that Jesus had said, as well as with Jewish monotheism. But all of these were strong challenges. In comparison, the scriptural proofs and interpretations Paul had offered seemed relatively weak. Yet Paul himself was not relying on scripture for his conclusion; he claimed *direct* revelation of this truth. And that put things on a very different plane.

How had the tillerman put it last evening when we were discussing how believers were persuaded? Ah yes: "You are relying on the testimony of other witnesses whose veracity you accept." How else could it be? Isn't that how we always come to acknowledge the truth of things we ourselves have not perceived? And I *did* accept Paul's veracity. Still, his revelation, a direct religious experience, was unique to him. Could he have been mistaken? Was this an instance of what Timothy had said at the beginning of our journey about those claiming special knowledge gleaned directly through supposed revelations from God, leading to modifications of the faith we have been taught? Certainly the testimony of *two* witnesses, traditionally required under Jewish law, was lacking; neither Timothy, nor Barnabas, nor Silas, nor anyone who worked with Paul had also claimed to have had such a direct revelation. Even the tillerman had observed that if a *common* perception were reported as the result of a religious experience—common among several who had it—then it should be accepted as true in the absence of some reason to think the perceivers were deluded or had a motive to fabricate their story. That commonality was lacking.

But despite his uncorroborated claim to divine revelation on the point, Paul had persuaded many thousands of believers that Jesus of Nazareth was indeed the literal Son of God, divine in every respect. He had all but persuaded me; if not for Peter's astute observations, I would not now be questioning the matter. How is it that Paul could be so persuasive? Was there a predisposition among his Gentile audience, free of the tradition of Jewish belief in one God, to accept the notion without also having to except a further mystery to explain its possibility? That could not be the entire reason for his success, for Paul had converted a number of Jews to his way of thinking as well. Was it simple charisma, nothing more?

I thought back to my discussions with Timothy while we were at sea—of how God's justice in requiring sacrifice for forgiveness of sin could be harmonized with His mercy and love if the sacrifice were of His own Son; of the analogy he drew to the filial sacrifice requested of Abraham on Mount Moriah; of the true meaning of the Eucharist as a means of actualizing the experience of union with God; of consumption of Jesus' blood, his life essence, leading to eternal life as the distinguishing quality of that essence. All of these things had felt so right to me at the time. Why had that feeling waned once I had heard Peter's perspectives?

It occurred to me that Timothy's conclusions on Jesus' divine sonship, which initially appealed to me as logical arguments from the ultimate logician, were in fact ultimately grounded in faith. In the end it was *Peter*, the simple fisherman, whose objections to those conclusions were grounded in logic. Timothy's efforts notwithstanding, Paul's theology could not be fully defended by pointing to evidence, nor by reason and logic, but only by faith. As someone who had struggled to harmonize faith and reason all his life, I finally had to accept that complete harmony was impossible. Timothy was surely right about one thing: if all of these conclusions were capable of logical proof, there would be no place for faith.

I felt paralyzed by my uncertainty, and by the fear of erring in so important a task as writing what could well become one of the definitive narratives of a fledgling church without any scriptural tradition uniquely its own. The thought that others who wrote after me might rely on my work and adopt the position I took on this issue weighed heavily on my mind. I desperately wanted God to solve this dilemma for me, to give me inspiration and direction. Why was He silent? Why, at so many crucial junctures in my life and at so many crises of my faith, had He remained silent?

Or was I just not listening closely enough?

With the sun setting outside my window, I seated myself at the desk in my room, placed a sheet of papyrus before me and picked up a reed-pen. Shutting my eyes, I tried to clear my head of all thoughts.

Then a picture began to form in my mind, a picture of a young lad wrapped in nothing but a sheet, hiding behind a tree on a moonlit night and watching a man being led away by torch-bearing soldiers, his hands bound behind him. Suddenly the flickering torchlight illuminated the prisoner's face, and once again I saw those piercing eyes, picking me out of the darkness, staring deep into my soul and holding me in their gaze. "*Know* me!" his eyes insisted. "You *know* me!"

But this time, I did not run away. With that rapturous, exquisite feeling of utter peace washing over me, I breathed in the cool evening air, opened my eyes, and began to write,

"*Here begins the gospel of Jesus Christ, the Son of God* . . ."

www.ingramcontent.com/pod-product-compliance
Lightning Source LLC
Chambersburg PA
CBHW071230170426
43191CB00032B/1225